D0900092

BY THE SAME AUTHOR

The Royal Navy Today
The Russian Convoys
British Sea Power
The Rescue Ships (with L. F. Martyn)
The Loss of the Bismarck

THE ATTACK ON
Taranto

VICE-ADMIRAL B. B. SCHOFIELD, CB, CBE

LONDON

IAN ALLAN

First published 1973

ISBN 0 7110 0421 8

© B. B. Schofield 1973

Published by Ian Allan Ltd, Shepperton, Surrey
and printed in the United Kingdom by
Morrison and Gibb Ltd, London and Edinburgh

Contents

Acknowledgements

The author wishes to thank all those who, in one way or another, assisted him with the writing of this book, particularly Rear-Admiral P. N. Buckley CB, DSO, the staff of the Admiralty Library, Captain C. L. Keighley-Peach DSO, OBE, RN and Captain F. M. Torrens-Spence DSO, DSC, RN and Major General G. N. C. Galuppini, Head of the Ufficio Storico della Marina Militare Italiana; also my daughter Victoria, who typed the manuscript.

B. B. Schofield

The author and publishers wish to thank all those who gave permission for quotations to be made in this volume from the books of which they hold the copyright, viz. The United States Naval Institute, Messrs Hutchinson and E. P. Dutton for the Estate of the late Admiral of the Fleet, Viscount Cunningham of Hyndhope, Messrs William Blackwood and Sons, the Societa Editrice Tirrena, and the Keeper of Navy Records, the Record Office.

The illustrations reproduced are by the courtesy of the Imperial War Museum, and the Historical Branch of the Italian Navy.

Introduction

It is not really surprising that there was a great deal of opposition to the introduction of aircraft into the Royal Navy. The Service had only recently adjusted itself to the revolutionary change from sail to steam and, at first, it appeared that here was yet another invention threatening to cause a new upheaval. So when, in March 1907, the Wright Brothers offered the Admiralty the opportunity of acquiring the patent rights of the flying machine in which, three years previously, they had made history by achieving the first sustained flight, it was politely declined. Almost alone amongst senior naval officers of that period, the First Sea Lord, Admiral Sir John (later Lord) Fisher realised the possibilities of this invention. A year later he sent an officer, Captain (later Admiral Sir) Reginald Bacon, to France to report on the first international air race which took place at Rheims. In that year Louis Bleriot flew across the Channel and Britain's insular security was breached. Fisher could see, in the ability to fly, a means of obtaining intelligence of the disposition of an enemy fleet both in harbour and at sea and it was natural that, at first, the lighter-than-air ship appeared more suited to this role than the heavier-than-air craft. The German Navy was of the same opinion and gave Count Zeppelin every encouragement with the development of the famous rigid airships named after him.

The first British naval airship was the 512 feet ($155\frac{1}{2}$ m) long *Mayfly*. She took two years to build but she had a life of only four months, being caught by a gust of wind and destroyed as she emerged from her hangar on September 29th 1911. The disaster somewhat damped the Navy's enthusiasm for aviation and it was due to two members of the newly formed Royal Aero Club, Francis McLean and C. B. Cockburn, who offered to lend the Admiralty aircraft and teach selected officers to fly, that the spark was rekindled. In response to a call for volunteers over 200 names were sent in, but only four were chosen, subsequently increased to five, and all gained the Royal

Aero Club's Aviator's certificate within six weeks of commencing training. Meanwhile another officer, Commander Schwann, who had been connected with the building of the ill-fated *Mayfly*, had bought an aircraft with private funds which he had fitted with floats and with which it was demonstrated that an airplane could take off and land on the water. The enthusiasm of these early aviators soon led to flights being made from special platforms erected on warships and also to the construction of seaplanes. The Admiralty, now impressed by all these activities, was moved to set out the duties which they considered naval aircraft should be capable of performing. These were:

(a) Reconnaissance of enemy ports;
(b) Reconnaissance of the area surrounding a fleet at sea;
(c) The location of submarines;
(d) The detection of minefields;
(e) Spotting the fall of shot for the guns of the fleet.

The year 1912 saw the beginning of the Naval Air Arm. In November of the previous year the Prime Minister, Mr Asquith, invited the Committee of Imperial Defence "to consider the future of aerial nagivation for both naval and military purposes; the means which might be taken to secure to this country an efficient air service; and also whether steps should be taken to co-ordinate the study of aviation in the Navy and the Army". A technical sub-committee, appointed to consider the matter, recommended that a single service be formed to be known as The Royal Flying Corps, which would comprise two wings, one naval and one military and the formation of an Air Committee of twelve members. A central pool of pilots was to be created, drawn from officers of both services, trained at a central school and available for duty with either of them. These recommendations were approved by Parliament on May 11th 1912.

The Admiralty at once objected to the interchangeability of pilots because of the very different conditions pertaining to operations over the sea and the land. Thanks to the eloquence of the First Lord, Mr Winston Churchill, the Cabinet was won over to the Admiralty's point of view and on July 1st 1914 the naval wing of the Royal Flying Corps, formally assumed the name by which it had already become known—The Royal Naval Air Service—and became an adjunct to the Royal Navy. While these deliberations had been in progress, the naval aviators had been considering the problem of bombing ships and flying off them under way, and they had made considerable progress with both of them. Also, thanks to Mr Churchill's ready support, the new service was steadily expanding, so that when war broke out in 1914, the RNAS could boast of seven airships, 52 seaplanes and 39 aircraft with a personnel strength of approximately 138 officers and 600 men. As the Royal Flying Corps was now part of the Army and would therefore have to accompany it to France, the RNAS was made responsible for the defence of Great Britain from air attack, a task for which it was not really suited and which later was partly responsible for its undoing.

Meanwhile, the Admiralty had discovered that seaplanes lacked the range to carry out their primary duty of scouting ahead of the fleet and in consequence would have to be carried in ships to the scene of operations. This led to the conversion of the old cruiser, HMS *Hermes*, and certain selected merchant ships into seaplane carriers. They were equipped with facilities for servicing the seaplanes and for hoisting them in and out. From the start, the German Zeppelins were made a priority target by the Government because of their ability to drop bombs on Britain and also because they were used by the German Navy for reconnaissance of the North Sea. As a result, plans were worked out for attacking the Zeppelins from both sea and land in their sheds in various parts of Germany. In order to reach some of the more distant ones RNAS aircraft were sent to Belgium from whence, after two unsuccessful attacks, they succeeded in destroying one, the Z.9, at Dusseldorf. An attack on Cuxhaven, although doing little damage, induced part of the German fleet to move to the Baltic. All in all the first four months of war vindicated the faith of those who believed that aircraft would be able to make a useful contribution to the war at sea, despite the fact that the German fleet had been somewhat coy in showing itself.

The Admiralty, to which Fisher had now returned as First Sea Lord, had, under his dynamic direction, embarked on an extensive programme of expansion of the RNAS, especially since the U-boat menace was beginning to make itself increasingly felt. It appeared that one way to get on top of it was to bomb the submarines in their lairs, but it was not long before it was discovered that such a form of attack was singularly ineffective. As an alternative, some small non-rigid airships were built to patrol the waters around the British coast in which the U-boats were operating. These, at least, had the effect of making it more difficult for the U-boats to operate on the surface and sink ships by gunfire, and it also enabled their positions to be reported so that surface craft could be sent to hunt them.

The Zeppelin raids on Britain once again focussed attention on the need to find ways and means of destroying them and the RNAS gained its first Victoria Cross through the action of Flight Sub-Lieutenant Warneford. While flying a Morane aircraft he destroyed LZ.37 in the air over Belgium. However it was apparent that seaplanes were not as suitable as land planes for attacking airships since they did not have as good a rate of climb, the secret of success being the ability to rise above the airship and attack it from there. The Commander in Chief of the Grand Fleet, Admiral Sir John (later Admiral of the Fleet Viscount) Jellicoe, was also asking for aircraft fitted with radio to scout ahead of the fleet, but, as mentioned, the poor endurance of the seaplane was a handicap and the available seaplane carriers were not fast enough to keep up with the fleet. In an endeavour to comply with his request, the Admiralty acquired a former Cunard passenger ship, the *Campania*, and fitted her with facilities for operating seaplanes, but two more years were to elapse before the problem of operating wheel-fitted aircraft from ships was to be solved satisfactorily.

Abroad the RNAS was adding to its laurels in support of operations at the Dardanelles and history was made when, on August 12th 1915, Flight Commander C. H. K. Edmunds, in a Short seaplane with a 14 inch (356 mm) torpedo slung under its fuselage, released it against a 5,000 ton Turkish supply ship lying off Injin Burnu. The ship listed and sank. The success was repeated in double measure five days later. On November 19th the Service gained its second Victoria Cross when Squadron Commander R. Bell-Davies, flying a single seater Nieuport aircraft, alighted in enemy territory and, under fire, successfully rescued the pilot of another aircraft which had been obliged to force land.

Another type of operation involving the use of aircraft took place off the coast of German East Africa where the cruiser *Königsberg*, after a brief cruise as a raider in the Indian Ocean, had taken refuge in the delta of the Rufigi River beyond the range of the guns of a watching British cruiser. She was ultimately destroyed by fire from shallow draft monitors assisted by spotting corrections passed from a Short seaplane brought from Bombay and flown by Flight Lieutenant J. T. Cull with Sub-Lieutenant H. J. Arnold as his observer.

The heterogeneous collection of aircraft, with which the RNAS was now equipped, was creating difficulties of maintenance and spare parts, and early in 1916, the Admiralty set about re-organising the whole service. It was decided to concentrate on three main types of aircraft, viz. a large bomber with a range of 300 miles, able to carry a bomb load of 500 lbs (227 kg); a fast single seater fighter with a high rate of climb and armed with a machine gun firing through the propeller; and a seaplane capable of carrying a torpedo. At the same time, attempts were to be made to design more powerful engines and better radio sets. Fortunately too, at this time, it was decided that the Royal Flying Corps should relieve the RNAS of responsibility for the air defence of Great Britain.

In March 1916, it was decided that an attempt should be made to discover and destroy the Zeppelin sheds thought to be located at Hoyer, a small town on the Schleswig-Holstein coast, opposite the island of Sylt. The seaplane carrier *Vindex* escorted by the Harwich Force of cruisers and destroyers was selected for the task and was supported by the battle-cruiser force. Although three out of five seaplanes, which took part in the attack, failed to return and the Zeppelin sheds were further inland at Tondern, the raid caused the High Seas fleet to raise steam and almost precipitated the fleet action which took place two months later off the coast of Jutland. In this action, which occurred on May 31st, the Germans had planned to use their Zeppelins but were prevented from doing so by the unfavourable weather conditions. Both the British Grand and Battle-cruiser Fleets had seaplane carriers attached to them. Just before the action began, the *Engadine*, attached to the former, launched a seaplane which sighted and shadowed a part of the German battle-cruiser force before being obliged to force land with a broken petrol pipe. Running repairs were made and the seaplane took off again but, by now, action had been joined and no further thought was given to air reconnaissance, although an early report of the position of the German battlefleet could well have altered the whole course of events. Due to not receiving the signal to raise steam, the Grand Fleet's seaplane carrier, *Campania*, left harbour too late to take any part in the action. However, the flight of the *Engadine*'s seaplane had demonstrated for the first time how valuable air reconnaissance could be in giving early information of the enemy's presence.

By the end of the year the RNAS had established itself as an integral part of the Royal Navy. This was recognised by the appointment on January 31st 1917 of an additional member of the Board of

Admiralty, known as the Fifth Sea Lord, with responsibility for all matters affecting naval aviation. This was the year which saw the appearance of the aircraft carrier proper. She was a merchant ship being built in England for Italy called the *Conte Rosso*, and was fitted with a flush deck forward for launching wheel-fitted aircraft and one aft for operating seaplanes. She was renamed HMS *Argus* and was to provide long and useful service extending into World War II. At the same time the fast armourless battle-cruiser, HMS *Furious*, had her foremost single 18 inch (457 mm) gun turret removed and a large flying deck with a hangar beneath built in its place. It was onboard this ship that, on August 3rd 1917, Squadron Commander E. H. Dunning DSC made the first ever landing of a wheel-fitted aircraft on a ship at sea. His death after repeating the achievement two days later was a tragedy for the RNAS but his feat was an historic one. It led to the adoption of the through deck, enabling aircraft to take off over the bows and land on over the stern. However, the problem of bringing them to rest satisfactorily and without damaging the aircraft was not solved for several years.

The successful aircraft designer, T. M. Sopwith, had been invited to submit a plan for an aircraft capable of carrying an 18 inch (457 mm) torpedo. In June 1917 he produced the Cuckoo, a single seater wood and fabric aircraft powered by a 200 HP Sunbeam Arab engine and capable of a speed of 98mph. It was the first wheel-fitted aircraft to be so armed. On trials it proved highly successful, but the first operational squadron did not join the fleet until October 1918 and so it was never tried out in action.

The public outcry resulting from the raids carried out with apparent impunity on Britain by the Zeppelin airships coupled with the appearance on the western front in France of German aircraft superior to anything possessed by the Royal Flying Corps and squabbles between the Navy and Army for the supply of aircraft, produced a crisis which called for immediate Government intervention. A committee under the chairmanship of the Prime Minister, Lloyd George, was set up to look into the matter. As his deputy, the Prime Minister selected Field Marshal J. C. Smuts, a member of the War Cabinet, statesman, soldier, philosopher and lawyer, but without any special qualifications for the task. Lord Milner, always ready with advice, wrote to him accusing the soldiers and sailors at the War Office and Admiralty of not grasping the fact that they were faced with a new kind of warfare, and "that, besides the help they have given the Army and Navy, the airmen will have to fight battles on their own". This did not accord with Generalissimo Foch's view that the first duty of fighting aeroplanes was to assist the troops on the ground and that air fighting was not to be sought except as necessary for the fulfilment of this duty. The Committee, after only four weeks of deliberation, came out with a recommendation that the RNAS and the RFC should be amalgamated into one service to be known as the Royal Air Force under a separate Ministry. In addition, there was to be "a small part specially trained for work with the Navy and a small part for work with the Army; these two small portions probably becoming, in the future, an arm of the older service". Although the hope was thus held out of a restoration of a separate naval air arm at some time, it was not realised without a long and bitter struggle, which lasted almost twenty years, between the Admiralty and the new Air Ministry.

It was evident that carrier design was an important factor in the future progress of naval aviation. In 1917 the Admiralty had taken over the Chilean battleship *Almirante Cochrane* of 22,000 tons which was building in Britain at Armstrong's shipyard on the Clyde. She was redesigned with an all-over flight deck and an island superstructure on the starboard side containing the bridge and wheel house—a complete innovation—which was to become standard practice in the majority of aircraft carriers. She was launched on June 8th 1918 and like the *Argus*, was to give many years of service under the name of HMS *Eagle*, until lost during World War II. At the same time, a contract was awarded to Armstrong's for the design of a carrier to be built as such from the keel upwards. Christened HMS *Hermes* she was only half the size of the *Eagle*, but she too gave nearly twenty years of service. The *Eagle* was commissioned in 1922 and the *Hermes*, a year later.

It was not long before the Admiralty and the Air Ministry found themselves at loggerheads over the training of personnel, the former being dissatisfied with the quality of the pilots allocated for duty with the Navy. Then came the Washington Treaty for the limitation of armaments, signed in 1922, and two years later the Admiralty took stock of the situation regarding the number of carriers and aircraft needed and their tactical employment. The three carriers, *Furious*, *Eagle* and *Hermes*, (the *Argus* was not regarded as operational) totalled 55,900 tons and the Treaty allowed Britain and the United States a total carrier tonnage of 80,000. In addition, any country was allowed, if it wished, to build two carriers of not more than 33,000 tons each. This clause had been agreed to allow the United States to convert the two battle-cruiser hulls, *Lexington* and *Saratoga*, to carriers, and Britain made use of it to convert the two fast battle-cruisers, *Courageous* and *Glorious*, in a similar manner. However it was not until 1928 that these ships joined the fleet and Britain still had 24,000 tons available to complete her quota. Due to stringent economy in defence expenditure the gap was not filled until 1936 when construction was begun on a new carrier, HMS *Ark Royal*, which was commissioned in 1938.

With regard to the aircraft, in 1924 the Fairey Flycatcher entered service as the standard single seater fighter and three years later the Fairey III F, a three seater spotter reconnaissance aircraft, was introduced. The Admiralty, again contrary to the Air Ministry, considered the torpedo as the best weapon with which to arm ship-borne strike aircraft, but its employment demanded a special type of aircraft. Since the Ministry did not see eye to eye with the Admiralty, (in their opinion the bomb was to be preferred), and it was responsible for the production of aircraft, it is not surprising that this requirement did not rank very high on its list of priorities. The Cuckoo's successor was the Blackburn Dart which entered service in 1923. It was a single seater aircraft and suffered from the grave disadvantage that the pilot, besides flying the aircraft, had to work out the right firing angle and also operate the release mechanism. Next came the Blackburn Ripon which entered service in 1929. A two seater, it was slightly faster and had a greater range than the Dart, although the rate of climb was not so good. The Ripon was succeeded by the Baffin and Shark, both of which offered only marginally better performance and their first line service was noticeably brief. In 1936 came the famous Fairey Swordfish. Although its performance was very little better than that of the Ripon and was not so good as the Shark, its magnificent handling qualities endeared it to all who flew it and it earned the respect of thousands of Fleet Air Arm pilots. They composed a song about it, the words of which were:

The Swordfish fly over the ocean
The Swordfish fly over the sea;
If it were not for King George's Swordfish
Where the 'ell would the Fleet Air Arm be?

Thus, on the outbreak of World War II in 1939, it was the standard

Torpedo-Spotter-Reconnaissance (TSR) aircraft in the British fleet. Compared with contemporary torpedo-carrying aircraft, such as the Douglas TBD.1 Devastator of the US Navy, (which had a maximum speed of 200 knots and a range of 985 miles, armed with a 1,000 lb torpedo) or the Naka BSN.2 (Kate) of the Japanese Navy (with a speed of 235 knots, a range of 1,400 miles, and 1,764 lb torpedo), the Swordfish, with a maximum speed of 125 knots, a range of 450 miles and a 1,200 lb torpedo, was obsolescent. Even its successor, the Albacore, with a speed of 155 knots and a range of 630 miles, was no match for its foreign competitors so that in the final stages of the war the Royal Navy's carriers had to be equipped with American aircraft. As regards the torpedoes themselves little had been done in the inter-war years to improve these very effective weapons. However a new pistol was designed which functioned both on impact and, if set to run under a ship, also as a result of the vessel's inherent magnetism. This as will be seen, was to play an important part in the story which follows.

In 1937 the Admiralty, thanks to the determination of the First Sea Lord, Admiral Sir Ernle (later Admiral of the Fleet Lord) Chatfield, regained administrative and operational control of the Fleet Air Arm. It had been a long, hard and at times embittered struggle and the victory was in a sense, a Pyrrhic one since, with another major war just around the corner there was insufficient time to make good the deficiencies which had resulted from twenty years of divided control. Fortunately, when in 1936 Germany's aggressive posture persuaded the British Government to sanction a certain amount of rearmament expenditure, orders were given to lay down two carriers of the Illustrious class (see Appendix 7) and the following year two more were ordered. In each of the 1938 and 1939 Navy Estimates provision was made for the construction of an improved Illustrious class carrier, with the result that on the outbreak of war in 1939 there were altogether six of these ships building, of which two had been launched, HMS *Illustrious*, on April 5th 1939 and HMS *Formidable* on August 17th, while a third ship, HMS *Victorious* took the water on September 14th, ten days after war was declared.

When, in September 1938, Hitler invaded Czechoslovakia, an action which led to the mobilisation of the British fleet, that part of it which was stationed in the Mediterranean and based in Malta, moved to its war base at Alexandria, Egypt. There the Commander in Chief,

Admiral Sir Dudley Pound, began preparations for attacking the Italian fleet, should Mussolini decide to rally to the support of his Axis partner in the event of war. At that time, the Mediterranean fleet included one aircraft carrier, HMS *Glorious* which was equipped with one squadron of Nimrod and Osprey fighters and three squadrons, each of twelve Swordfish TSR aircraft. Under her Commanding Officer, Captain A. L. St G. Lyster CVO, RN, these squadrons had been brought to a very high pitch of efficiency as a result of constant practice. Lyster, who features again in this story, was a gunnery specialist, but he appreciated that there was a great future for naval aircraft, an opinion reinforced by experience in his present command. A heavy jowled man with a sardonic sense of humour, he inspired confidence in his subordinates, whose problems he readily shared and understood. Yet he could be tough when the occasion demanded. Admiral Pound, who had arrived in 1935 to take over command of the Mediterranean at the time of the crisis caused by Mussolini's invasion of Abysinnia, recollected that, at that time, a plan had been worked out using Fleet Air Arm aircraft for an attack on the Italian fleet in its main base at Taranto. Captain Lyster had located a copy of this plan in his ship's secret files when he took over command, so he was not in the least surprised when Admiral Pound sent for him one day and told him to bring it up to date. After going over it with his Commander (Flying) and Senior Observer, he was able to report back to the Commander in Chief that, despite the growing strength of the Italian Air Force (Regia Aeronautica), he was confident that, if surprise could be achieved, the odds were in favour of dealing the enemy a crippling blow. After what has been said about the general attitude of senior naval officers to the Fleet Air Arm, the initiation of this plan is all the more remarkable. It shows that there were some forward thinking officers who visualised the potential striking power of aircraft and their ability to exploit the vulnerability of ships to attack by torpedo. As an American Admiral is credited with saying apropos of bombing versus torpedo attack "It's much more effective to let water in through the bottom than air through the top".

In the event, as is well known, the Munich crisis ended by Britain and France buying time at the cost of Czechoslovakia's independence. The plan for the attack on the Italian naval base at Taranto was put back in the safe, where it remained until events once again called for its reconsideration.

PART I

CHAPTER ONE

The Mediterranean 1939–1940

In September 1939 Hitler's savage assault on Poland, the independence of which Britain and France had guaranteed, made war with Germany inevitable, but Mussolini, for all his braggadocio and sabre-rattling, opted for neutrality, thus raising faint hopes in diplomatic quarters that he would prefer discretion to valour. In consequence, the British Mediterranean fleet which, on the outbreak of war, comprised three battleships, one aircraft carrier, three 8 inch (203 mm) gun cruisers and three 6 inch (152 mm) gun cruisers, an A/A cruiser, 26 destroyers, four escort vessels, ten submarines and four minesweepers, found itself being gradually milked of ships in order to meet other commitments.

However, following Germany's successful attack on France and Italy's assumption of an increasingly threatening posture, it became imperative to reconstitute this fleet in order to ensure the containment of the Italian fleet and the control of the eastern basin. The situation was aggravated when, after Mussolini's declaration of war on June 10th, eleven days later France signed an armistice with the Axis powers and the French fleet ceased to be available for ensuring the security of the western basin. Another force had therefore to be assembled in haste at Gibraltar, known as Force 'H' to take over this responsibility. Moreover, during the early months of the war, Britain had lost two of the six carriers with which she began the war, and of the four remaining, only one, the *Ark Royal*, was a modern ship. This deplorable situation was only mitigated by the knowledge that new carriers, the construction of which was referred to earlier, were shortly coming into service.

In redisposing the fleet to meet the new situation, resulting from a hostile Italy, the Admiralty allocated the carrier *Eagle* to the reconstituted Mediterranean fleet commanded by that redoubtable Scot and magnificent leader Admiral Sir Andrew Cunningham. She joined his flag from Eastern waters towards the end of May 1940.

But even though the Italian fleet lacked aircraft carriers, Italy's geographical position in the central Mediterranean enabled her fleet to operate over a wide area under cover of the shore-based aircraft of the Regia Aeronautica whereas Admiral Cunningham had only the *Eagle*'s eighteen Swordfish TSR aircraft to pit against the enemy's entire air force. These were later supplemented by three Gladiator fighters, and, in the absence of pilots trained to fly them, the *Eagle*'s Commander (Flying), Commander C. L. Keighley-Peach RN, and two volunteer Swordfish pilots trained by him, successfully kept the Regia Aeronautica at bay until the arrival of HMS *Illustrious*. It was not possible, at that time to count on any air support from the fortress of Malta, the pre-war planners having written it off as indefensible, a policy only reversed literally at the eleventh hour, but too late to be of any use at this stage.

The Chiefs of Staff of the Italian Armed Forces were given their first intimation that 'il Duce' had decided to enter the war on the side of Germany, whenever he considered the moment opportune, on April 9th 1940. The Chief of the Italian Naval Staff was Admiral Domenico Cavagnari who also held the post of Under Secretary of State for the Navy. Had he not been extremely able and a prodigous worker, he would not have been able to wear these two hats as successfully as he did. Unfortunately for him policy was formulated by the Supreme Command, dominated by Mussolini and the Army, neither of whom understood the conduct of maritime warfare. Cavagnari replied to Mussolini's intended declaration of war in a memorandum of some length. He pointed out the difficulties arising from his country's unfavourable geographical position and the impossibility of achieving any sort of surprise action when entering a war already in an advanced stage. He foresaw that Britain and France would either take up positions at each end of the Mediterranean and await Italy's exhaustion or they would adopt a more aggressive strategy leading to encounters between the opposing fleets, in which substantial losses would be incurred by both sides. Assuming they adopted the first alternative, it would be difficult to carry out offensive operations with surface forces and, as regards submarine warfare, poor results were likely since merchant shipping in the Mediterranean would be virtually non existent. The outcome of the second course of action would be that, while the Allies could replace their losses from ships surplus to their needs, Italy could not and the fleet would thus be thrown on the defensive and all possibility of pursuing important strategic objectives designed to defeat the opposing naval forces would be forfeited. This led him to the conclusion that a decision to enter the war did not seem justified given the prospect of being obliged to adopt a defensive maritime strategy.

He went on to state the factors adverse to the operation of Italian naval forces which were (a) the shortage of reconnaissance aircraft and the difficulty of having to rely on the co-operation of the Air Force and (b) the poor state of the anti-aircraft defences at the naval bases. He concluded his memorandum with these prescient words: "Whatever character the war in the Mediterranean assumes, in the end our naval losses will be substantial. In the subsequent peace negotiations Italy would emerge not only without territorial pledges, but also minus a fleet and perhaps an Air Force".* In this realistic way he forecast the course of events as regards the Italian Navy during the forthcoming conflict.

Like the British Admiralty in London, the Italian Naval High Command had a well equipped Operations Room in the Ministry of Marine, known as Super Marina, to which access was only obtainable by holders of a special pass. It was linked with all the naval commands in Italy and Sicily by a rapid communications network which functioned throughout the twenty-four hours and was capable of handling a very large number of incoming and out-going messages satisfactorily. On large maps were shown the positions of all Italian warships and merchant ships, as well as those of any enemy ships reported or the position of which could be deduced from intercepted British messages. Like the German Navy, the Royal Italian Navy began the war with a great advantage, conferred by the ability to decypher British naval messages. In view of the inadequacy of the air reconnaissance provided by the Regia Aeronautica, this was often the only intelligence available of the movements of British ships.

In June 1940, the Italian fleet comprised the two modernised battleships *Giulio Cesare* and *Conte di Cavour*, each armed with ten 12·6 inch (320 mm) guns, nineteen cruisers, seven of which were armed with 8 inch (203 mm) and twelve with 6 inch (152 mm) guns, 61 fleet destroyers, 69 destroyers and torpedo boats, 105 submarines and a number of minelayers, patrol vessels, and motor torpedo boats.

* La Guerra sui Mari—Tome I, pp. 166–8 by Admiral Bernotti.

Two old battleships, *Caio Duillio* and *Andrea Doria*, were undergoing modernisation and two new ones were completing. Italy had an agreement with her Axis partner, Germany, that each country's Navy would have complete liberty of action in its own theatre of operations. Mussolini followed up his declaration of war on June 10th 1940 with a directive calling for "the offensive at all points in the Mediterranean and outside". However Admiral Cavagnari held to his original concept of pursuing a defensive policy. This, he defined as closing the Adriatic and Tyrhenian Seas to enemy forces and the maintenance of the important line of communications between metropolitan Italy and both Libya and the Dodecanese islands in the Aegean. At the same time, he envisaged offensive raids by high speed forces against French lines of communication with North Africa, possible attacks by high speed torpedo craft on ships in harbour and minelaying off enemy ports. Until France withdrew from the conflict on June 22nd, the combined Anglo-French fleets in the Mediterranean were superior to that of Italy except in destroyers and submarines, but afterwards, the need for some of the tasks envisaged by Cavagnari was eliminated. Nevertheless, there was no change in the general policy cited above, although there was a notable increase in activity, especially in the number of convoys being despatched to Libya.

Even though the Army had originally said that it had sufficient supplies in Libya for six months, as soon as the fighting started, urgent requests poured in for all kinds of stores and equipment. These convoys generally had a strong escort of destroyers and a covering force of battleships and cruisers. In July, during one of these operations, an encounter took place with the British Mediterranean fleet under Admiral Cunningham, during which a 15 inch shell fired by HMS *Warspite*, struck the battleship *Giulio Cesare*, flying the flag of Admiral Inigo Campioni, Commander in Chief of the Italian fleet, causing severe damage. As a result of this he broke off the action and returned to port, taking advantage of his superior speed. Campioni complained that he had not received sufficient support from the Regia Aeronautica. Reconnaissance had proved inadequate and the results of the bombing attacks on the British fleet, during which no hits were obtained, were most disappointing, especially since, at that time, it was without fighter aircraft defence. To make matters worse, the Italian ships themselves had been attacked by their own aircraft, despite every possible means being used to disclose their identity.

The operations are described at some length in the Italian Official History. What impressed their Naval Staff most was the advantage conferred on the British fleet by the presence of an aircraft carrier, which "besides permitting them to fight off the activities of our aircraft, both bombers and reconnaissance, allowed the enemy to carry out attacks with torpedo aircraft, which, although frustrated by ships manoeuvring, interfered with the formations attacked and so delayed their rejoining the remainder of our forces".★

A further blow to Italian morale was administered ten days later, when, on July 19th, HMAS *Sydney* and a division of destroyers encountered two six inch gun cruisers, the *Giovanni delle Bande Nere*, flying the flag of Vice Admiral F. Casardi, and the *Bartolomeo Colleoni*. The last named was sunk after a spirited action, in which the only damage received by the British force was a hit on the *Sydney*'s funnel. Admiral Casardi was taken by surprise, since he was expecting air reconnaissance from the Dodecanese islands, which did not materialise, and he had not ordered either ship's aircraft to be catapulted in lieu to carry out a dawn reconnaissance of the area ahead of his two ships. Captain Novaro of the *Colleoni* was rescued, although, seriously wounded, he died subsequently at Alexandria, where he was buried with full military honours.

On August 2nd the Italian fleet was reinforced by the arrival of the two new battleships, *Vittorio Veneto* and *Littorio*, each with a main armament of nine 15 inch (381 mm) guns, which could outrange all the 15 inch gun battleships in the British fleet except for the *Warspite* and *Valiant*, which had been modernised. The Italian ships were also much faster. At the end of August the work of modernising the *Caio Duillio* was completed and so, on August 31st, Admiral Campioni took his fleet to sea. It comprised two new and three modernised battleships accompanied by ten cruisers and 34 destroyers. Its object was the interception of an inferior British force comprising two battleships, the carrier *Eagle*, five light cruisers and nine destroyers. The British force was covering a convoy from Alexandria to Malta and, at the same time, meeting the long awaited reinforcements from England, which included the new carrier, HMS *Illustrious*, and the battleship *Valiant*. The two fleets approached to within 90 miles of each other at dusk on August 31st and Admiral Cunningham

★ "The Italian Navy by Commander M. A. Bragadin, Italian Navy, in World War II" p. 33. US Naval Institute.

regarded action at dawn the next day as certain. However, to his surprise, Campioni reversed the course of his fleet during the night and returned to his base at Taranto. His action is explained by Commander Bragadin as being due to a severe storm which blew up during the night and which prevented reconnaissance aircraft from obtaining any information on the position of any of the British forces. It also made the going heavy for his destroyers, which, in any event, were running short of fuel, and so, in the afternoon of September 1st, the Italian High Command, Supermarina, ordered all ships to return to base.[*]

The newly commissioned carrier, HMS *Illustrious*, was a valuable addition to Admiral Cunningham's fleet. She was commanded by Captain (later Admiral Sir Denis) Boyd DSC, RN, a senior officer of great experience who had earned his decoration while serving as a Lieutenant in the light cruiser, HMS *Fearless*, which led the First Destroyer Flotilla into action at the Battle of Jutland during World War I. Although a torpedo specialist, he had taken a keen interest in naval aviation throughout his career and, as a young officer, had privately learned to fly. A man of medium height, he was possessed of great physical and moral courage and quickly gained the complete confidence of his ship's company. The *Illustrious* was of a new design of carrier with an armoured flight deck and included, amongst her complement of aircraft, twelve fighters, four of which were new eight gun Fairey Fulmars. Her strike aircraft comprised two squadrons, each of twelve Swordfish TSR aircraft. However, despite this addition to the strength of his carrier-borne aircraft, Admiral Cunningham described the air situation as 'unsatisfactory' because of the lack of reconnaissance aircraft capable of monitoring the movements of the Italian fleet. The flying boats operating from Malta and Alexandria "were too slow and too vulnerable" he has recorded. "The Italians, on the other hand, had full knowledge of our movements."[†] The *Illustrious* reached Gibraltar on August 29th and sailed the following day to rendezvous with Admiral Cunningham's fleet south of Malta. She was flying the flag of Rear Admiral A. St L. Lyster, former Captain of HMS *Glorious*, who had been appointed Rear Admiral, Aircraft Carriers, Mediterranean. It is not surprising that, on hoisting his flag, Lyster should have instructed his

[*] Ibid., p. 33.
[†] "A Sailor's Odyssey" by Admiral of the Fleet Viscount Cunningham, KT, GCB, OM, DSO, p. 267.

staff to examine anew the plan he had drawn up two years previously for an attack on the Italian fleet at Taranto. By the time he reached Alexandria he had refreshed his memory with the details and was in a position to discuss the operation with his Commander in Chief.

During the month of August the first aircraft to be equipped with torpedoes joined the Italian Air Force. The war had already demonstrated their value and at long last the pleadings of the Navy were heeded. There were, however, only about fifty of them and the training of the crews took some time. Although they were very much an arm calling for close naval co-operation they were placed under Air Force control.

On September 13th, Marshal Graziani, Commander in Chief of the Italian forces in North Africa, launched an offensive with the object of invading Egypt, and this kept the British fleet busy supporting the defending army. However, to everyone's surprise, having reached Sidi Barrani, the Marshal halted his forces and instructed them to dig in. The Royal Navy, thus released from its task, was able to give consideration to other pressing matters, included in which was the attack on the Italian fleet in its base. Meanwhile, an essential requirement of such an attack had been met, that of adequate and continuous reconnaissance of Taranto harbour, including photographs from which the scale of the defences could be determined. A week after the *Illustrious* had joined the fleet, three American built Glenn Martyn aircraft, later known as Marylands, reached Malta and took over reconnaissance duties from the Sunderland flying boats. These aircraft were part of a consignment ordered by France in the United States for use as long range bomber/ reconnaissance aircraft. They were crated and on their way when France fell, and fortunately redirected to England, where they were turned over to the Royal Air Force, which, lacking any really high speed aircraft of this type, was delighted to have them. Since the War Cabinet considered Admiral Cunningham's need to be the greatest, the first three to be assembled were ordered to form No 431 General Reconnaissance flight and to proceed to Malta, after familiarisation and night flying trials which were carried out under great difficulty because of enemy air activity. The flight commander was Squadron Leader E. A. Whitely, an experienced and capable pilot, well endowed with the qualities of resourcefulness and courage which work of this nature calls for. On arrival at Luqa, one of Malta's battle-scarred airfields, they were immediately assigned to the task of photographing ports in Italy and Sicily, as far north as Naples and as far east as Brindisi, as well as searching for enemy shipping on the supply route between Italy and ports in North Africa, and also in the Ionian Sea. In addition, they were ordered to pay daily visits to enemy naval bases, especially at Taranto.

The art of photographic interpretation was not fully developed until the latter stages of World War II, but shortly before the *Illustrious* joined the Mediterranean fleet, RAF Middle East Command in Cairo had set up an interpretation unit. The photographs taken by the Marylands were therefore flown there for study. Admiral Lyster's Assistant Staff Officer Operations, Lieutenant David Pollock RNVR, obtained permission to undergo a five day course with this unit, when his ship first reached Alexandria. His peace time profession was that of lawyer, but his favourite hobby was sailing, a combination admirably suited to the duties on which he now found himself engaged. He furnished himself with a stereoscope by means of which two pictures of the same area, when placed side by side and examined through it, produced a three dimensional effect. Taking into account shadows, these enabled an observer to deduce information not noticeable in an ordinary photograph. The knowledge he acquired during this short course was to prove invaluable later on.

At the end of September another and less favourable opportunity occurred for Admiral Campioni to bring the British fleet to action, when a force comprising the two modernised battleships, *Warspite* and *Valiant*, with the aircraft carrier *Illustrious* in company, once again sailed into the central Mediterranean during an operation designed to cover troop reinforcements for Malta. The force was sighted off Sidi Barrani and Admiral Campioni sailed to intercept it with a force of four battleships, which included the *Littorio* and *Vittorio Veneto*. However, air reconnaissance failed to locate the British force until the afternoon of October 1st, when it was seen to be heading back for its base at Alexandria. Aircraft from the carrier had sighted the Italian ships 120 miles to the northward, but as the primary object of the British force on this occasion was the safe arrival of the troops at Malta, it did not seek action with the Italian fleet, which returned to base. Soon afterwards, the whole British fleet returned to the area while covering a supply convoy to Malta, but this time the Italian reaction was to send out a small force of destroyers to carry out a night torpedo attack on the British fleet.

They made contact with the 6 inch gun cruiser *Ajax*, which sank three of them and damaged a fourth while receiving seven shell hits, none of which caused serious damage.

Although, during the first five months of the war with Italy, the British fleet or detachments of it, made some sixteen sweeps into the Central Mediterranean from its base at Alexandria, the only encounters with the Italian fleet were those mentioned above. However, the generally defensive policy adopted by the Italian fleet enabled it to dominate the waters around Malta, and not only made it more difficult for supplies to reach the beleaguered island, but also hindered the attempts of British forces to impede the passage of the Italian convoys carrying much needed supplies to their armies in North Africa. Logical though this policy was, it had one inevitable consequence, that of heightening the morale of the British fleet in a way that nothing else could have done, and to the extent that it was ready and willing to overcome the quite formidable problems involved in attacking the Italian fleet lying in its strongly defended base of Taranto.

CHAPTER TWO

Operation MB.8—Prelude to Judgement

Whenever the opportunity arose, the air crews of the two carriers, *Illustrious* and *Eagle*, carried out intensive training including night flying in order to equip themselves for the hazardous enterprise, which they were certain they would shortly be called upon to undertake. By mid October, Lyster was able to report to the Commander in Chief that he considered they were sufficiently well trained, and it was decided that the attack should take place on Trafalgar Day, October 21st. However, an unfortunate mishap onboard the *Illustrious* necessitated a postponement. Down in the ship's hangar long-range tanks were being fitted to the Swordfish aircraft to increase the distance at which they could be launched from their objective. As already mentioned, these aircraft had a range of only 450 miles, which was insufficient since it was desirable that the attack should be delivered from a position in which the carrier was unlikely to be detected. As a result, a 60 gallon tank was being secured by metal straps in the Observer's seat in each torpedo-carrying aircraft. This meant that the air gunner had to be left behind and the Observer himself, besides being seriously incommoded, ran the risk of being drenched with petrol from the tank overflow pipe as the aircraft accelerated for the take off. One of the fitters on the job suddenly slipped and fell, and, in so doing, the screwdriver which he was clutching brushed across a pair of live electric terminals in the aircraft's cockpit. The spark ignited some petrol dripping from a tank which had not been properly drained and started a fire which spread swiftly to the surrounding aircraft. Fire-fighting parties leapt into action, the overhead spray extinguishers of the drenching system were switched on and in a few minutes the blaze died down. However, brief though it had been, the incident had serious repercussions. Two of the Swordfish were destroyed and five others had been drenched with salt water. It was at once evident, that, even if they worked around the clock, it would not be possible to ready the two Swordfish squadrons by the chosen date.

As every experienced commander knows, the unexpected permeates all operations of war, and on top of the situation described above, Admiral Cunningham now had to face a more serious one. On October 28th, Italy delivered an ultimatum to Greece, the terms of which were rejected by that country, which appealed to Britain for help. Immediate steps were taken to respond to this request and Admiral Cunningham was instructed to establish a fuelling base for the fleet and for aircraft at Suda Bay in Crete, whence troops and stores could be assembled and transported to the Piraeus. Italian attempts to interfere with these measures were unsuccessful but their implementation added to the other tasks which the Mediterranean fleet was called upon to undertake at this time. These included the escort of convoys to and from Malta and the passage through the Mediterranean of reinforcements comprising a battleship, two cruisers and three destroyers, all of which had embarked military personnel for the garrison of Malta.

Reconnaissance of Taranto harbour on October 27th had revealed that the Italian main fleet was there. It comprised five battleships, three 8 inch gun cruisers, six 6 inch gun cruisers and a number of destroyers. It was therefore well placed to interfere with operations which the British forces were now about to undertake and to which the code name of Mike Bravo Ate (MB.8) was given. It is an indication of Admiral Cunningham's ability to size up his opponent's reaction, that the final phase of this complex operation was to be the postponed attack on the Italian fleet in Taranto harbour. The conditions of moonlight were favourable for this any night between November 11th and 19th. It might well be thought that so much activity in the central Mediterranean would have sent the Italian fleet hurrying out to sea to do battle with an enemy, who had the temerity to intrude again on what Mussolini regarded as his exclusive preserve, but, as will be seen, the British Commander in Chief's intuition was to be proved right and 'Judgement', the code name given to that particular part of the operation, was singularly apt.

Before sailing to carry out Operation MB.8, another unforeseen event necessitated an amendment to that part of it dealing with the intended attack on Taranto. The 22 year old carrier *Eagle*, as a result of the bombing attacks and near misses, to which she had been subjected during the July operations, developed a serious defect in her petrol supply system. Only a major refit in a dockyard could make this good and so there was no question of her being able to take part in the operation. It was therefore decided that she should transfer five of her Swordfish aircraft and eight complete crews to the *Illustrious* to give her a striking force of 24 aircraft. This was six less than originally planned, but, as will be related later, an accident caused the number to be still further reduced.

Meanwhile, Rear Admiral Lyster had despatched Lieutenant Pollock in a Swordfish aircraft to Cairo to obtain the latest intelligence on the situation at the Italian naval base. A series of excellent photographs covering the entire harbour were available, from which the positions of the battleships, cruisers and destroyers lying there could be noted, and also those of the gun emplacements ashore, established for their defence. However, what at first puzzled the Admiral's staff officer was a series of small white blobs on all the prints, and which were clearly not blemishes. Together with the Royal Air Force expert, Flight Lieutenant John Jones, he examined and re-examined them—then an idea struck him—could the mysterious spots be barrage balloons like those being used for the defence of London? In planning Operation 'Judgement' no allowance had been made for obstructions of this kind; the method of attack would therefore need to be revised if his guess was correct. First, it was necessary to acquaint both Admiral Lyster and the Commander in Chief, but the Royal Air Force could not see its way to part with the photographs. Pollock was not a man to be outdone, and so when no one was looking he 'borrowed' them for 24 hours, hoping they would not be missed. Back at Alexandria he showed them to Admiral Cunningham's Chief of Staff, Rear Admiral (later Admiral of the Fleet Sir Algernon) Willis, who agreed with his interpretation of the new hazard. He then returned to the *Illustrious* to have the pictures copied and the following day he flew back to Cairo and replaced the unmissed photos in their folder. After requesting that official confirmation of this important piece of intelligence be sent to the Commander in Chief, he returned onboard his ship to await events. In due course, the report came through, but, thanks to the advance information he had obtained, a revised plan of attack had already been prepared for submission to Admiral Cunningham before the fleet left harbour.

The magnitude of Operation MB.8 can be gauged from the fact that it involved six separate forces totalling five battleships, two carriers, ten cruisers, thirty destroyers and three trawlers. The second carrier was the *Ark Royal* belonging to Force 'H' based on Gibraltar, flying the flag of Vice Admiral Sir James Somerville, but which could not take part in the attack on Taranto, since she was required to provide air cover for the passage of ships through the western basin of the Mediterranean.

There were four convoys to be escorted, MW3, of five merchant ships, from Alexandria to Malta, to which three ships were added, loaded with guns and ammunition for the base at Suda Bay. The second one, AN6, comprised three ships carrying petrol and fuel from Egypt to Greece; the third one, ME3, contained four ships returning empty from Malta to Alexandria, while the fourth one included empty ships returning to Alexandria from Greece and Turkey. During the operation, the battleship, *Barham*, with the cruisers *Berwick* and *Glasgow* were to be escorted from Gibraltar by Force 'H' to rendezvous with Admiral Cunningham south of Malta as reinforcements for his fleet.

The operation was timed to commence on November 4th with the sailing of convoy AN6 from Alexandria. The following day, the Malta bound convoy, MW3, sailed and overtook AN6 off the southern entrance to the Kaso Strait. As they passed through it and north of Crete, the two ships for Suda Bay were detached en route, and from there, through a position 40 miles south of Cape Matapan, the convoy steered for its destination. Admiral Cunningham, in the battleship *Warspite* with the *Valiant*, *Malaya*, *Ramillies*, the carrier *Illustrious*, the cruisers *Gloucester* and *York* and an escort of destroyers, sailed from Alexandria at 1300 on November 6th and steered to the westward. By noon on the 8th, the fleet was half way between Crete and Malta, when convoy MW3 was sighted, ten miles to the south-westward. The fleet took station to the northward, in order to be in a position to intercept any Italian warship attempting to attack it. At 1230, MW3 was sighted by Italian reconnaissance aircraft, which were driven off by fighters launched from the *Illustrious*. The fleet had now approached to within 180 miles of Sicily and air attacks could be expected at any time. Another reconnaissance aircraft appeared at 1520 but was chased away by the vigilant fighters. About an hour later seven S.79 bombers appeared and were attacked by three Fulmar fighters, which shot down two, whereupon the remaining five jettisoned their bombs and made off. At 0900/9 the battleship *Ramillies* was detached with an escort of three destroyers

to accompany the convoy to Malta, while the rest of the fleet proceeded to a covering position about 100 miles to the south-eastward of the island. The cruisers were ordered to sweep northward and search for enemy forces as the weather was too overcast for air searches to be relied upon. During the latter part of the forenoon and the afternoon, enemy aircraft were reported in the vicinity of the fleet four times and at 1604 a Cant 506 shadowing aircraft was shot down by a Fulmar. The Italians, now aware of the presence of British forces to the west and east of Malta, were trying unsuccessfully to obtain a picture of the situation. On November 9th, Commander Bragadin says "it was learned that the Gibraltar force had reversed course in keeping with the now classic British operational procedure. As far as the eastern squadron was concerned, the reconnaissance service gave various and conflicting reports. By that evening Supermarina could only conclude, in a general way, that this British force must have been about 300 miles from Taranto and on its way to Alexandria at approximately 1500 that afternoon".*
The mistake was not discovered until the following day.

Meanwhile, at 1219 the *Illustrious* had launched a Swordfish aircraft on a routine anti-submarine patrol, but shortly after taking off, the engine failed and it forced landed in the sea close to the *Warspite*, the crew being rescued by a destroyer. At 0700/10 another Swordfish, launched to carry out reconnaissance of a sector between north-west and north-east from the fleet, crashed soon after take off. Although the crew was rescued, the aircraft was lost, reducing the number available for the attack on Taranto to 22. Three hours later the battleship *Barham* and her two accompanying cruisers were met, the latter being detached to land the troops they were carrying, at Malta. At Noon, in a position some 40 miles west of that island, enemy aircraft again made contact with the fleet and one of them, a Cant 501, was shot down. At 1330 ten enemy bombers attacked the fleet in two formations from a height of 14,000 feet (4,297 m) and dropped 25 bombs without scoring a hit. They were intercepted by the *Illustrious*'s Fulmars and one was damaged. The fleet now turned eastward and at Noon/11, had returned to a position about half way between Malta and Crete, but meanwhile another Swordfish had mysteriously crashed. It had climbed to 1,500 feet (457 m) when the engine cut out without warning and it landed in the sea. The Pilot,

* Commander Bragadin: ibid, p. 44.

Sub-lieutenant Alistair Keith and his Observer, Lieutenant George Going, managed to inflate their life-saving dinghy and climb into it before being rescued by a boat from the cruiser *Gloucester*. Going, who has been described to the author by an officer who knew him as 'the bravest man I ever met' suddenly realised that unless he could get back to the *Illustrious*, he would miss the raid on Taranto. He went up to the cruiser's bridge to put the matter before the Captain who proved sympathetic and gave orders for the ship's amphibious Walrus aircraft to be catapulted off and return the two aviators to their ship.

Commander James Robertson RN, the Commander (Flying) onboard the carrier, known to his shipmates as 'Streamline' for his remarkable ability to speed up any operation connected with the handling of aircraft, was determined to discover the reason for the loss of the three Swordfish in such unusual circumstances. They all belonged to Number 819 squadron and this suggested contamination of the fuel rather than individual engine failures. He ordered the tanks of the remaining nine aircraft of the squadron to be drained immediately and the fuel examined. This done, it was found to contain water and sand mixed in with the petrol as well as a peculiar fungus type growth festooning the baffles in the tanks. Further inquiry elicited the fact that they had all been refuelled from the same supply point in the hangar and this pointed to contamination of one of the ship's tanks. This, he surmised, might well be the result of the action necessary to extinguish the fire, or possibly some other cause. However, whatever it might have been, the important thing was to have discovered it and to have been able to prevent what would have been little short of a disaster so far as the impending attack on Taranto was concerned.

It had been arranged that simultaneously with the attack on the Italian fleet base, light forces under the command of Vice Admiral Pridham Wippell should carry out a sweep into the mouth of the Adriatic. This force was detached to proceed in execution of previous orders at 1310/11 and at 1800 the *Illustrious*, escorted by the cruisers *Gloucester*, *Berwick*, *Glasgow* and *York*, also separated from the main body of the fleet preparatory to the launching of Operation 'Judgement'.

CHAPTER THREE

The Plan of Attack

The port of Taranto, at the head of the Gulf of that name, is situated in the heel of Italy, 520 miles from Malta. It was the Italian fleet's premier base and contained all the facilities necessary to support ships of all types. It comprised an Inner harbour known as Mar Piccolo, completely landlocked, to which access was obtained through a narrow channel called the Canal, and a large Outer harbour known as Mar Grande. The latter was enclosed by a submerged breakwater extending south-westward from Cape Rondinella to the island of San Pietro and continuing thence to the Isolotto San Paolo, which marked the northern side of the 1,298 yard (1,187 m) wide entrance. To the southward, a breakwater, known as the Diga di San Vito, extended north-eastward for 1,760 yards (1,609 m) from a position on shore 1,319 yards (1,206 m) north-eastward of the Cape of that name. The Italian High Command was well aware of the possibility of an air attack on the harbour and had taken extensive precautions to protect the ships within it. These included the positioning of 21 batteries of four inch (102 mm) guns, thirteen of which were ashore and eight mounted on floating rafts. There were also 84 heavy and 109 light machine guns sited to cover the whole area of the port. Although perhaps adequate in number, the batteries consisted of out of date weapons and they were not equipped for night barrage fire. The 22 searchlights were modern but only two of them were linked with the airphonic listening posts, of which thirteen had been established in suitable positions in the country surrounding the harbour area. Additional illumination was to be provided by two searchlights from each ship. Of the 13,998 yards (12,800 m) of anti-torpedo net defence required to protect the ships in the Outer harbour, only 4,593 yards (4,200 m) were in position; a further 3,171 yards (2,900 m) was ashore waiting to be laid. The fact that this had not been done was due to objections by some senior naval officers who believed that they would interfere

Admiral of the Fleet Viscount Cunningham of Hyndhope KT, GCB, OM, DSO, Commander in Chief, Mediterranean 1939–1941.

Above: Captain (later Admiral Sir) Denis Boyd KCB, CBE, DSC, Commanding Officer, HMS *Illustrious* (1940–41).

Left: Vice Admiral Sir Lumley St G Lyster KCB, CVO, CBE, DSO, Flag Officer (Air) Mediterranean, in conversation with Captain Ian Robertson RN.

Right: Vice Admiral Sir Henry Pridham Whippel KCB, CVO, Vice Admiral 2nd in command Mediterranean Fleet 1939–1941.

Far right: Admiral Domenico Cavagnari, Royal It Navy, Chief of Naval Operations 1938–40.

Above: Admiral Inigo Campioni, Royal It Navy, Commander in Chief, Italian Fleet 1939–40.

Right: Admiral Arturo Riccardi, Royal It Navy, Admiral Commanding Taranto 1940, who succeeded Cavagnari as Chief of Naval Operations.

Left: Admiral Angelo Iachino, Royal It Navy, who succeeded Campioni as Commander in Chief, Italian Fleet 1940.

Below: HMS *Illustrious*, aircraft carrier, after commissioning August 1940.

HMS *Eagle*, the Mediterranean
fleet's only aircraft carrier until the
arrival of HMS *Illustrious* in August
1940.

A Fulmar fighter coming in to land
on the carrier's deck.

A Fairey Swordfish aircraft armed
with an 18 inch torpedo.

A Glenn Martin Maryland reconnaissance aircraft used to take
photographs of Taranto harbour
before and after the attack.

The Italian battleship *Vittorio Veneto* damaged during the attack.

The Italian battleship *Andrea Doria* present in Taranto but undamaged.

with the movements of ships entering and leaving harbour. To complete this quite imposing array of defences, a barrage of some 90 balloons had been installed, but, as luck would have it, bad weather during the first week in November had destroyed 60 of them and only 27 were in position on the night of the attack. Ten were moored to rafts just west of an inner breakwater, known as the Diga di Tarantola, which jutted out into the Mar Grande for 2,625 yards (2,400 m) and about the same distance to the north-eastward of the Diga di San Vito. A further ten were sited ashore in a line extending north-eastward from the inshore end of the Diga di Tarantola and the remaining seven were moored to rafts in the middle of the northern half of the Mar Grande on a line running north-eastward towards the northern shore of the harbour (see plan 1). There was, however, one serious lacuna in the defences, and that was the absence of any smoke-making apparatus.

On November 11th the following ships of the Italian fleet were moored in Taranto harbour. In the Mar Grande, the two 15 inch (381 mm) gun battleships, *Vittorio Veneto* and *Littorio*, and the four 12·6 inch (320 mm) gun battleships, *Cavour*, *Giulio Cesare*, *Caio Duilio* and *Andrea Doria*. The last named ship had been unable to recover her stern moorings on her return to harbour. Also present were the 8 inch (240 mm) gun cruisers *Zara*, *Fiume* and *Gorizia*, and the destroyers, *Folgare*, *Baleno*, *Fulmine*, *Lampo*, *Alfieri Gioberti*, *Carducci and Oriani*. In the Mar Piccolo, at buoys, were the 8 inch (204 mm) gun cruisers *Trieste* and *Bolzano* and the destroyers, *Granatiere*, *Alpino*, *Bersagliere* and *Fuciliere*, while moored stern to the jetty were the 8 inch (204 mm) gun cruisers *Pola* and *Trento*. In addition, there were the 6 inch (154 mm) gun cruisers *Garibaldi* and *Abruzzi*, and the destroyers *Freccia*, *Strale*, *Dardo*, *Saetta*, *Maestrale*, *Libeccio*, *Grecale*, *Scirocco*, *Camicia Nera*, *Geniere*, *Lanciere*, *Carabiniere*, *Corazziere*, *Ascari*, *Da Recco*, *Usodimare* and *Pessagno*. Also in the Inner harbour were five torpedo boats, sixteen submarines, four minesweepers, one minelayer, nine tankers, supply ships and hospital ships as well as some tugs and merchant ships.

The ships were berthed in a manner considered to afford them the best production from the kind of attack considered likely. The repeated visits by British reconnaissance aircraft had not passed unnoticed and were regarded as an indication that air attacks were being planned. As a result, at nightfall ships assumed a state of complete readiness with main armaments half manned and A/A guns fully so. In the event of an alarm all men on watch had orders to take cover while those not on duty were to proceed below.

The Admiral in charge of the port was Arturo Riccardi, a man who took his responsibilities very seriously. He fully appreciated the risk of an air-borne torpedo attack on the ships lying in the Outer harbour, but he counted on receiving adequate warning of the approach of hostile aircraft. He believed that a carrier approaching within striking distance was almost certain to be sighted by reconnaissance aircraft before she could reach a position from which she would be able to launch her aircraft. The Italian Army, on the other hand, which was responsible for the A/A batteries, was less confident about the security of the base and would have been glad to see the fleet move to one further north, such as Naples. Admiral Campioni, however, was reluctant to forego the strategic advantages of Taranto vis a vis his hope of cutting off the supplies with which, despite his efforts, the British were managing to keep Malta going.

The original plan of attack on Taranto, as conceived by Rear Admiral Lyster had had to be considerably modified as a result of the discovery of the barrage balloons, the anti-torpedo nets, the fewer aircraft available due to the *Eagle* not being present and finally the loss of three more Swordfish, as related above. In its final form, the plan was as follows: the *Illustrious* and her escort of cruisers and destroyers would steer for a position 'X', 270° 4 miles from Kabbo Point, Cephalonia, in order to pass through it at 2000 on November 11th. This early hour had been chosen to minimise the risk of attack by surface craft, which was considered to be greater than that of detection by reconnaissance aircraft, which, as events were to prove, were hardly ever allowed to approach the fleet by the vigilant Fleet Air Arm fighters. Since only 21 Swordfish aircraft were available instead of the 30 previously envisaged, they were organised in two flights of twelve and nine aircraft respectively, six of which in each flight were armed with torpedoes and the remainder with bombs. The first strike of twelve aircraft would be launched on reaching position 'X', which was so chosen that the aircraft would not have to fly more than a total distance of 400 miles. Since the balloon barrage and the anti-torpedo nets restricted the number of favourable dropping positions, the bombing aircraft would be equipped with flares. The second strike of nine aircraft would be launched an hour after the first one, i.e. at 2100. It was hoped to commence the recovery of the first strike at about 0100/12 in a position 20 miles

270° from Kabbo Point. Moonrise was at 1543 and at 2300 it would bear 197° at an altitude of 52° as seen from Taranto. The first strike was to fly up the centre of the Gulf and approach the harbour from the south-west. The six bombing aircraft would illuminate the target area by dropping flares along its eastern edge before proceeding to bomb the cruisers and destroyers lying in the Mar Piccolo.

This, in broad outline, was the plan as given to the Pilots and Observers onboard the *Illustrious* and on which the respective Squadron Commanders then proceeded to work out, in greater detail, the specific method of attack each would adopt.

To carry out an aircraft torpedo attack by day in the open sea is a difficult enough task, as was confirmed on many occasions during the war, but, although a ship in harbour is a sitting duck, if the harbour is well defended and under conditions of darkness, the difficulties are enormously increased. Not only does such an attack call for a cool head and steady nerves, but good judgement is also essential, since reliance has to be placed on the eye as opposed to instruments. The first thing is to identify the target and decide on the method of approach. However thorough the planning and the briefing, this is something which can only be decided on the spur of the moment. The dive down to water level must bring the aircraft to the right place for dropping with a clear range. If there is a balloon barrage, course must be adjusted to miss it or to pass between two of the balloons and no attention must be paid to A/A fire. Reliance cannot be placed on the altimeter in choosing the moment to pull out of a dive, since it suffers from time lag, and so it is a question of experience and making use of the known height of the target to assist one's judgement. The aircraft must be aimed straight at the target and must be level in both axes before the torpedo is released or it will not run straight. Finally, the range at which the torpedo is dropped must not be less than 300 yards (275 metres) as the safety range on the pistol will not have been run off and the warhead will not explode even if a hit is obtained. Just before dropping and when climbing for the getaway, the aircraft is most vulnerable, and since modern warships are capable of devastating close-range fire, the chances of survival cannot be assessed as other than poor.

A Swordfish aircraft had been sent to Malta earlier in the day to collect the latest pictures of Taranto taken by the invaluable Maryland reconnaissance aircraft. These, Lieutenant Commanders K. W. Williamson and J. W. Hale, the leaders of the first and second strikes, now began to study carefully. They were excellent photographs, taken on a clear day from a height of only 8,000 feet (2,438 m) and five Italian battleships could be clearly seen and so could the unwelcome white blobs of the barrage balloons. The fear that the enemy ships might put to sea before the attack took place was allayed when, during the evening, a patrolling Sunderland aircraft keeping watch against this possibility, not only reported that all ships were present and that there was no sign of an impending departure, but also that a sixth battleship had joined the other five. This was indeed good news. Williamson decided on an approach with his squadron to the harbour at a height of between eight and ten thousand feet (2,438–3,048 m). He would then glide down with two torpedo-armed aircraft of the leading sub-flight across the Diga di Tarantola from the westward, while the other sub-flight would come in from the north-west. By attacking from two directions he hoped to confuse the A/A defences, but in any case each pilot was free to take whatever action the situation demanded, especially should the A/A fire prove more formidable than expected or the balloon barrage interfere with the approach. Hale chose to approach in line astern from the northwest. He estimated that this would give his flight a better run in as well as a more certain chance of hitting, since, from this angle, the battleships overlapped one another. The disadvantage of an approach from the north-west was that his aircraft would have to pass unpleasantly close to the A/A batteries sited on either side of the Canal connecting the Inner and Outer harbours and they would have to cross the line of barrage balloons moored to lighters to the north-west of their targets. However, on balance, it was considered that these risks were acceptable. The balloons were about 300 yards (273 m) apart and the wingspan of a Swordfish was less than 48 feet (14·6 m) so that the chances of passing between two without touching the wires were roughly ten to one in favour.

The average depth of the anchorage where the battleships lay was 49 feet (15 m) and the torpedoes with which the Swordfish were to be armed and on which the success of the attack depended, were the standard 18 inch (457 mm) Mark XII set to run at 27 knots at a depth of 33 feet (10 m). They were fitted with Duplex pistols which the *Illustrious* had brought from England and which had only come into service shortly before the outbreak of war. They differed from the ordinary contact pistols in that they included a device actuated by an enemy ship's magnetic field as the torpedo passed underneath her and which fired the primer and exploded the warhead. Since the bottom of a ship is more vulnerable, being less well protected, than the sides, the use of these pistols, it was hoped, would increase the effectiveness of the attack. However, they still had some faults which had not been eliminated when they were brought into service, one of which was a tendency to explode prematurely when running in a swell. Fortunately in the case of the attack on Taranto, such conditions were unlikely to be encountered, but two other problems presented themselves. To minimise the risk of a torpedo being dropped at too steep an angle and hitting the bottom before being able to take up its preset depth, the aircraft must be in level flight or very slightly nose down at an altitude of 150 feet (45 m) when the weapon is released. The depth of water on dropping must not be less than six fathoms (11 m) and the distance from the target must be greater than 300 yards (274 m) as a safety device prevents the pistol from being actuated until the torpedo has run that distance. The first problem could only be overcome by the skill of the Pilot, but the second could be mitigated to some extent by running off some of the safety range before loading the torpedo in the aircraft. Although this entailed a certain amount of risk, it was readily accepted by the aircraft crews.

The bomb-carrying aircraft were armed with six 250 lb (112 kg) semi-armour piercing bombs, but those detailed for flare dropping only carried four bombs in addition to sixteen flares.

The extent of Operation MB.8 and the number of British forces operating in the Central Mediterranean appears to have confused the enemy. According to Commander Bragadin, who was serving in Supermarina at the time, it was known that both the Gibraltar and Alexandria forces were at sea, the latter reported as comprising three battleships (it was in fact four) and a carrier, and believed to have left their respective bases on November 7th. As a result, the fleet at Taranto had been brought to short notice for steam. The results of air reconnaissance the following morning (November 8th) were negative but during the afternoon a convoy was sighted steering towards Malta, outside the range of possible interception. A little later Admiral Cunningham's covering force of battleships was sighted to the south of the convoy, steering south. Nine more submarines in addition to the normal patrols were ordered to the area and a number of motor torpedo boats were ordered to patrol the Malta Channel. Twenty-five bombers took off from Sicilian

CHAPTER FOUR

The Attack Goes In

"When detached, *Illustrious* will adjust course and speed to pass through position 'X' at 2000"—so ran the orders of Rear Admiral Lyster to the carrier's Commanding Officer. They continued: "On completion of flying off first range, course will be altered 180° to starboard, speed 17 knots and a second alteration of 180° to starboard will be made to pass again through position 'X' at 2100, when course and speed will be adjusted as before." As the bows of the carrier sliced through the calm Mediterranean sea, flanked on either side by the cruisers *Gloucester*, *Berwick*, *Glasgow* and *York* with four destroyers, down below in the hangar, the aircraft fitters were carrying out final checks on the 21 Swordfish aircraft on which the success or failure of the operation depended. All aircraft are allotted an identification number; those of the *Illustrious* bore the letter 'L' while those lent from the *Eagle* carried the letter 'E'. With their wings folded they presented a curious sight, but this was necessary to enable them to be stowed in the limited space available and accommodated on the lift which carried them up to the flight deck. Before this took place, each Pilot would inspect his aircraft, check the controls, test the torpedo dropping gear and make sure that all the equipment was in full working order. He made sure that the emergency rations were onboard as these were part of the escape plan for any Pilot or Observer who had the misfortune to be shot down. The Observers went up to the Air Intelligence Office for a last minute briefing and a final look at the photographs of the stronghold they were about to attack. To them, as navigators, was assigned the important task of guiding their aircraft during its four-hour flight to and from the target and of finding the carrier again—a tiny dot on a darkened sea. Fortunately they had the black mass of the island of Cephalonia, off which they knew the carrier would be steaming, to help them, and once within 50 miles of the carrier, they should be able to pick up her homing beacon. There was of course the possibility, which could not be allowed for, that the carrier might be intercepted by enemy forces and be unable to make the prearranged rendezvous, but that was an added risk which had to be taken just like that of being shot down, and something to be pushed to the back of the mind and not discussed.

The First Attack
At 1945 the *Illustrious* increased speed to 28 knots and the great ship shuddered as down in the engine room the Artificers on watch opened up the valves, admitting steam to the turbines, while in the boiler rooms additional burners were switched on to generate the extra power required. The Commander Flying took up his position in a special sponson just below the bridge from where he had a full view of the darkened flight deck and the dimly discernible figures moving about it. In reply to his querulous enquiry concerning the readiness of the first flight for take off, he was told that there had been a slight delay in fuelling. Then, just as eight bells struck in muffled tones over the ship's broadcasting system, the last of the twelve Swordfish came up the forward lift and was ranged beside the other eleven. The warning klaxons were sounded, engines were switched on, Pilots and Observers, now clad in bulky Sidcot suits and Mae Wests, clambered into their aircraft and fastened their parachute harness with the help of the fitters. Engines were revved up, oil pressures checked and the readings of the many dials in the cockpit scanned by practised eyes. The Observers put on the earphones of their radio sets and erected their chart boards and navigational equipment. The Intercom with the Pilot was plugged in and communications tested. The flash of a green shaded torch from the leading aircraft told Robertson that it was ready for take off. He passed the information to Captain Boyd who, disguising the intensity of his feelings, gave the order to Carry On, in a matter of fact voice. A green light flashed from Flying Control, the fitters and rigger, lying prone on the deck, whipped away the holding chocks and one by one the pilots opened their throttles, causing their aircraft to speed along the flight deck, now outlined in fairy lights, and up into the surrounding darkness.

The first disturbance of that quiet November night at Taranto was at 1955 when a diaphonic listening post picked up the sound of aircraft somewhere to the south of the harbour. The information was passed to Command Headquarters, where it did not generate much interest as it could well have been just another reconnaissance aircraft. However, about ten minutes later a number of other airphonic stations began sending in reports of suspicious noises, and so the Fortress Commander was informed and he ordered the Alarm to be sounded. The crews manned their guns while the civilian population hurried down to the air-raid shelters. An A/A battery opened fire but soon ceased and the listening posts reported the sound of aircraft engines to be fading. The intruder appeared to have turned away and after a short pause the All Clear was sounded and peace returned, but not for long.

Three quarters of an hour later further reports came from the airphonic stations on the eastern arm of the Gulf of suspicious noises and another Alarm was sounded. The cause of all the trouble was, in fact, the Sunderland aircraft from Number 228 Squadron, Middle East Command, carrying out its important duty of patrolling the Gulf and watching for any movement on the part of the Italian fleet. Once again the disturbing sounds died away and quiet again descended on the city of Taranto and the darkened ships lying within its capacious harbour.

At 2225 the telephones in Command Headquarters started ringing again and 25 minutes later the sleeping inhabitants were awakened by a third Alarm. As the noise of aircraft engines coming from the south-east intensified, expectancy rose. Suddenly the batteries in the San Vito area erupted in flame while orange and red tracers patterned the sky. The curtain had risen on what will always be remembered by the Italians as 'Taranto Night'.

Flying at a speed of 75 knots and a height of 7,500 feet (2,286 m), eight of the twelve Swordfish of 815 Squadron had at last risen clear of the cloud in four sub-flight V formations of three aircraft, and the Flight Commander, Williamson, was able to take stock of the situation. The four missing aircraft, which had obviously lost touch during the climb, included one torpedo armed and three bombers. He was not unduly concerned about the last named whose mission called for independent action anyway, but he sincerely hoped that no misfortune had overtaken the missing torpedo aircraft. The time was 2115 and his Observer, Lieutenant Norman Scarlett, reckoned that there was still an hour and a half to go. At about 2250, Williamson saw the sky ahead illuminated by bursts of gunfire as the batteries guarding Taranto put up a protecting barrage against the unseen enemy aircraft detected approaching, thus confirming visually the accuracy of Scarlett's navigation. Several of the other aircraft crews noted the firework display with which they were being welcomed and deduced that the enemy had not been caught napping.

Williamson and Scarlett, in aircraft L4A, with Sub-Lieutenants Macaulay and Wray in aircraft L4R and Sub-Lieutenants Sparke and Neale in aircraft L4C, led the flight up the Gulf of Taranto. The weather was fine and clear with a light surface wind, but at 8,000 feet (2,438 m) it was westerly 10 knots. The sky was 8/10ths covered with thin cloud and the moon was 3/4 full, bearing about 190°. As they approached, they spotted the missing torpedo aircraft L4M, piloted by Lieutenant Swayne with Sub-Lieutenant Buxall RNVR as his Observer. Having lost touch with the remainder, he had made straight for the target and, arriving half an hour early, had passed the time orbiting above it and keeping the defenders guessing what it was all about. The moment had now come to detach the flare droppers. These were aircraft L4P, with Lieutenant L. J. Kigell RN as Pilot and Lieutenant H. R. B. Janvrin RN as Observer, and L5B, the Pilot being Lieutenant C. B. Lamb RN with Lieutenant K. G. Grieve RN as Observer. They were detached to seaward of Cape San Vito, from where a stream of shell intermingled with tracers now began to pour from the batteries. Both aircraft were flying at a height of 7,500 feet (2,286 m) and at 2302 L4P began dropping a line of magnesium flares at intervals of half a mile in a north-easterly direction to the south-eastward of the line of barrage balloons, which were protecting the landward side of the anchorage. They were set to burn at 4,500 feet (1,371 m). Having completed his task satisfactorily, Kigell turned to starboard and, after cruising around for about quarter of an hour, he made a dive-bombing attack on the oil storage depot a quarter of a mile inland from the anchorage, but results were not observed. L4P then set course to return to the *Illustrious*. L5B, the stand-by flare dropper, finding that the flares dropped by L4P were functioning correctly, followed the sub-flight leader and joined in the bombing of the oil depot before turning for home.

Williamson, in L4A with L4C and L4R in company, flew to the centre of the Mar Grande. The A/A fire was now intense and appeared to be concentrated in a cone over the centre of the harbour. He put his aircraft into a shallow dive, heading straight for the inferno erupting below him. He had three and a half miles to go to reach the battleships moored in the eastern part of the harbour. Losing height rapidly, he passed between two of the barrage balloons moored just west of the Diga di Tarantola, narrowly missing one of them, and then on over the breakwater towards the destroyers *Lampo* and *Fulmine*, which engaged him at almost point blank range. Suddenly the massive hull of the battleship *Conte di Cavour* loomed up ahead and Williamson pressed the release button for his torpedo, and the aircraft, relieved of the weight, jerked upwards. He banked steeply to starboard and, as he did so, a burst of automatic machine gun fire ripped into his aircraft, which plummeted straight into the sea. However, his torpedo had found its mark and a few minutes later the great battleship was shaken by a violent explosion beneath her keel between the conning tower and 'B' turret. The other two aircraft of the sub-flight, L4C and L4R, crossed the breakwater at a height of only 30 feet (9·1 m) amidst a hail of fire. They were hoping to attack the *Vittorio Veneto*, but were too far south and, sighting the *Conte di Cavour*, they dropped their torpedoes at a range of about 700 yards (640 m) from her. Unfortunately, they both missed and the torpedoes ran on to explode spontaneously close to the battleship *Andrea Doria*, without however damaging her. After dropping, L4C banked sharply to port and both aircraft set course to return to the carrier.

The second sub-flight leader, Lieutenant N. McI. Kemp RN in L4K with Sub-Lieutenant (A) R. A. Bailey RN as his Observer, passed north of San Pietro Island at a height of 4,000 feet (1,219 m). The batteries, both on the island and on Cape Rondinella to the northward, kept up a continuous fire on him, but miraculously his aircraft passed through it unscathed. The enemy battleships close inshore were clearly silhouetted against the light of the slowly descending flares. Diving steeply, Kemp passed around the northern end of the balloon barrage and fortunately, just at that moment, the A/A fire of the nearby cruisers temporarily ceased. Skimming low over the water, he pointed his aircraft at the battleship *Littorio* and, when the range had dropped to an estimated 1,000 yards (914 m), he released his torpedo. His mission accomplished, he had just time to see the silver streak of his weapon below him heading towards its target, before putting his aircraft into a steep climb, pursued by a hail of tracer bullets. Skilfully avoiding the southern group of barrage balloons, he gained the open sea. His torpedo hit the *Littorio* on her starboard bow.

Swayne in L4M, who, it will be remembered, had arrived early and had been obliged to await the arrival of the rest of the strike, followed his sub-flight leader Kemp in L4K north of San Pietro

Island, but at a height of only 1,000 feet (305 m) and steered straight for the northern end of the breakwater. Intense A/A fire was encountered from the ships and batteries as he crossed the harbour, losing height. On reaching the end of the mole he made a sharp turn to port and let go his torpedo 400 yards (365 m) from the *Littorio*, which it struck on the port quarter only a few seconds after the hit obtained by L4K's torpedo on the starboard bow. However, Swayne could not wait to see the results of his attack, and, lifting his aircraft up and over the masts of the battleship, he banked to port and fled from the scene pursued by a hail of flak.

The last of the torpedo-armed aircraft of the first strike was E4F, with Lieutenant M. R. Maund RN as Pilot and Sub-Lieutenant (A) W. A. Bull RN as Observer. The former, who alas lost his life on January 11th 1943 during air operations off Malta, has left us this dramatic account of his part in the attack. "Six thousand feet. God, how cold it is here! The sort of cold that fills you until all else is drowned, save perhaps fear and loneliness. Suspended between heaven and earth in a sort of no-man's land—to be sure, no man was ever meant to be here—in the abyss which men of old feared to meet if they ventured to the ends of the earth. Is it surprising that my knees are knocking together? We have now passed under a sheet of alto-stratus cloud which blankets the moon, allowing only a few pools of silver where small gaps appear. And, begob, Williamson is going to climb through it! As the rusty edge is reached I feel a tugging at my port wing, and find that Kemp has edged me over into the slipstream of the leading sub-flight. I fight with hard right stick to keep the wing up, but the sub-flight has run into one of its clawing moments, and quite suddenly the wing and nose drop and we are falling out of the sky! I let her have her head and see the shape of another aircraft flash by close overhead. Turning, I see formation lights ahead and climb up after them, following them through one of the rare holes in this cloud mass. There are two aircraft sure enough, yet when I range up alongside, the moonglow shows up the figure 5A—that is Olly. The others must be ahead. After an anxious few minutes some dim lights appear amongst the upper billows of the cloud, and opening the throttle we lumber away from Olly after them. Poor old engine—she will get a tanning this trip.

"The sub-flight is reassembled now at 8,000 feet. We have come to the edge of the cloud. The regular flashing of a light away down to starboard claims attention. 'There's a flashing light to starboard,

Bull, can you place it?' 'Oh, yes' and that is all—the poor devil must be all but petrified with the cold by now.

"Then the coast appears. Just a band of dull wrinkled greyness. Bull arouses himself from his icicles enough to be able to tell me that we have roughly 40 minutes to go, and I enough to remind him to close the overload tank cock before we go in. But we make no turn to get out to seaward again; instead we shape our course parallel to the coastline, not more than five miles away, giving away in one act any chance of surprise we might have hoped for.

"Years later. Some quaint-coloured twinkling flashes like liver-spots have appeared in the sky to starboard. It is some time before I realise their significance; we are approaching the harbour; and the flashes are HE shells bursting in a barrage on the target area. We turn towards the coast and drop away into line astern, engines throttled back. For ages we seem to hover without any apparent alteration; then red, white, and green flaming onions come streaming in our direction, the HE bursts get closer, and looking down to starboard I see the vague smudge of a shape I now know as well as my own hand. We are in attacking position. The next ahead disappears as I am looking for my line of approach, so down we go in a gentle pause, glide towards the north-western corner of the harbour. The master switch is made, a notch or two back on the incidence wheel, and my fear is gone, leaving a mind as clear and unfettered as it had ever been in my life. The hail of tracer at 6,000 feet is behind now, and there is nothing here to dodge; then I see that I am wrong, it is not behind anymore. They have shifted target; for now, away to starboard, a hail of red, white, and green balls cover the harbour to a height of 2,000 feet. This thing is beyond a joke.

"A burst of brilliance on the north-eastern shore, then another and another as the flare-dropper releases his load, until the harbour shows clear in the light he has made. Not too bright to dull the arc of raining colour over the harbour where tracer flies, allowing, it seems, no room to escape unscathed.

"We are now at 1,000 feet over a neat residential quarter of the town where gardens in darkened squares show at the back of the houses marshalled by the neat plan of streets that serve them. Here is the main road that connects the district with the main town. We follow its line and, as I open the throttle to elongate the glide, a Breda swings round from the shore, turning its stream of red balls in our direction. This is the beginning. Then another two guns farther north get our scent—white balls this time—so we throttle back again and make for a black mass on the shore that looks like a factory, where no balloons are likely to grow. A tall factory chimney shows ahead against the water's sheen. We must be at a hundred feet now and soon we must make our dash across that bloody water. As we come abreast the chimney I open the throttle wide and head for the mouth of the Mar Piccolo, whose position, though not visible, can be judged by the lie of the land. Then it is as all hell comes tumbling in on top of us—it must have been the fire of the cruisers and Mar Piccolo Canal batteries—leaving only two things in my mind, the line of approach to the dropping position and a wild desire to escape the effects of this deathly hailstorm.

"And so we jink and swerve, an instinct of living guiding my legs and right arm; two large clear shapes on our starboard side are monstrous in the background of flares. We turn until the righthand battleship is between the bars of the torpedo sight, dropping down as we do so. The water is close beneath our wheels, so close I am wondering which is to happen first—the torpedo going or our hitting the sea—then we level out, and almost without thought the button is pressed and a jerk tells me the 'fish' is gone.

"We are back close to the shore we started from, darting in and out of a rank of merchant ships for protection's sake. But our troubles are by no means over; for in our darting shither and thither we run slap into an '*Artigliere*' class destroyer. We are on top of her fo'c's'le before I realise that she hasn't opened fire on us, and though I am ready for his starboard pom-pom, he has a sitting shot at something between 50 and 100 yards. The white balls come scorching across our quarter as we turn and twist over the harbour; the cruisers have turned their fire on us again, making so close a pattern that I can smell the acrid smoke of their tracer. This is the end—we cannot get away with this maelstrom around us. Yet as a trapped animal will fight like fury for its life, so we redouble our efforts to evasion. I am thinking 'Either I can kill myself or they can kill me' and flying the machine close down on the water wing-tips all but scraping it at every turn, throttle full open and wide back.

"With a shock I realise that we are clear of the worst of it anyway. Ahead is the island that lies between the horns of the Outer Harbour, a low black mass that, at our speed of 120 knots, is suddenly upon us. We blithely sail by its western foot, oblivious of what it may contain, when comes the tearing sound of shell as red balls spurt from a position no more than a hundred yards away, passing close ahead of us. Away we turn to starboard, then, as the stream grows, round to port again, and so we zig-zag out into the open sea. . . . At last we are free to climb. At 3,000 feet it is cool and peaceful, a few shining clouds casting their dark shadows on the sea and the warm orange cockpit light showing up the instruments that must tell me all is well. All we have to do now is to get back and land on, thoughts that worry me not at all".* After this brilliantly delivered attack, it is sad to have to record that his torpedo, alas, missed its target and exploded on hitting the ground on the *Littorio*'s starboard quarter at about 2315.

Meanwhile, the four bomb-armed Swordfish were carrying out their part in the attack. E5A, with Captain O. Patch RM as Pilot and Lieutenant D. G. Goodwin RN as Observer, arrived over San Pietro Island at 2306 at a height of 8,500 feet (2,590 m) and headed for the Mar Piccolo where his targets, the enemy cruisers and destroyers moored stern to the jetty, were lying. In the midst of the smoke and flame from the A/A gunfire which surrounded them, they were difficult to distinguish, but at last he saw them and dived to attack. When down to almost masthead height, Patch flattened out and let go his six bombs, then turned east. Unfortunately no hits were obtained, but as he made good his escape over the peaceful Italian countryside he noticed a large fire burning a mile and a half east of where the ships were moored.

Aircraft L4L, with Sub-Lieutenant (A) W. C. Sarra RN as Pilot and Midshipman (A) J. Bowker RN as Observer, crossed the enemy coast to the west of Taranto at a height of 8,000 feet (2,438 m) and dived down to 1,500 feet (457 m) over the Mar Piccolo. Unable to pick out his target, he passed over the dockyard and suddenly spotted the hangars and slipways of the seaplane base right ahead. Appreciating that these would make an excellent secondary target, he came down to 500 feet (152 m) and released his bombs. A large explosion resulted and the hangars burst into flames. Belatedly the batteries and machine guns in the vicinity opened fire, but they did not prevent L4L from successfully disengaging to the south.

Aircraft L4H, with Sub-Lieutenant (A) A. J. Forde RN as Pilot with Sub-Lieutenant (A) A. Mardel-Ferreira RNVR as Observer, had lost contact with the main group and reached the area east of Cape San Vito just as Kiggell, L4P, started to drop his flares. Forde arrived

* Excerpt from *A Taranto Diary* by Lieutenant M. R. Maund, DSC, RN, in Flying Tales from Blackwoods, Series 1.

over the Mar Piccolo just as Sarra, L4L, was circling in search of his target. He picked out the ships lying stern to the jetty and looking like 'sardines in a tin' as he later described them. He let go his bombs from a height of 1,500 feet (457 m) but no hits were observed. Being uncertain whether or not his bombs had released, he went round and repeated the attack before breaking away to the north-west and crossing the coast five miles north of the harbour. Despite intense A/A fire from the enemy warships his aircraft was undamaged.

The last of the bombers E5Q, with Lieutenant J. B. Murray RN as Pilot and Sub-Lieutenant (A) S. M. Paine RN as Observer, followed L4H to the east of Cape San Vito and on to the Mar Piccolo, bombing the line of ships and running across them on an east-west course at a height of 3,000 feet (914 m). One bomb hit the destroyer *Libeccio* but failed to explode. Murray then turned 180° to port and withdrew on the opposite course to the one on which he had approached. By 2335 the last aircraft of the first strike had withdrawn but the hornets' nest had been so stirred up that the guns continued to fire, putting up a barrage in all four sectors of the defence perimeter long after the sound of the departing aircraft had died away.

The Second Strike

At 2120 the *Illustrious* again turned head to wind and the second strike, led by Lieutenant Commander J. W. Hale RN of 819 Squadron with Lieutenant G. A. Carline RN as his Observer, began to take off. This time things did not go with the faultless precision of the first strike's launching. Seven of the nine aircraft had taken off successfully and the eighth, L5F, began to move towards the centre line of the flight deck when the ninth and last, L5Q, also began to taxi forward from the opposite side. The two aircraft met and their wings locked. Engines were cut while fitters and riggers rushed forward to disentangle them. L5F's main plane had had some of its fabric torn off and several of the wing ribs were broken, but L5Q was undamaged. A consultation between Captain Boyd and Commander Robertson ensued and it was decided to allow L5Q to take off, but L5F would have to be struck down for repairs. By this time Hale had begun to wonder what had happened to his two missing aircraft; then a recount made the number eight and soon after a signal on a shaded lamp told him to 'Carry On' and so he knew that something had happened to L5F. It was now 2145.

The eight aircraft in 'V' formation had been flying east for twenty

48

Above and below:
Photographs of part
of the Italian fleet
lying in Taranto on
September 28 1940.

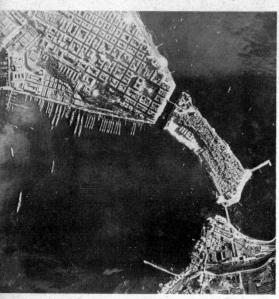

Left: Photograph of Taranto harbour showing the Canale and ships berthed stern to the wall in the Mar Picolo.

Below: An etching by the artist Roland Langmaid showing HMS *Illustrious* parting company from the fleet prior to the attack.

Photograph of Taranto harbour after the attack showing the damaged battleship *Caio Duilio* beached and listing to starboard.

Another view of the Italian battleship *Caio Duilio* after the attack.

The Italian battleship *Caio Duilio* with upper deck awash after the attack.

Left: A meeting between Grand Admiral Raeder, Chief of the German Naval Staff, and Admiral Arturo Riccardi, Chief of the Italian Naval Staff, on February 19 1941.

Below: A Ju 87 dive bomber of the German Air Force of the type used to attack HMS *Illustrious* in January 1941.

Left: Bombs bursting around HMS *Illustrious* during the attack on her on January 10th 1941.

Below: A near miss off *Illustrious*'s port bow.

Above: Scene on *Illustrious*'s flight deck looking aft during the attack.

Right: A near miss off the port side forward.

Right: A bomb bursting in the sea off the starboard beam of HMS *Illustrious.*

Below: Scene during the attack on *Illustrious* in Malta harbour on January 16 1941.

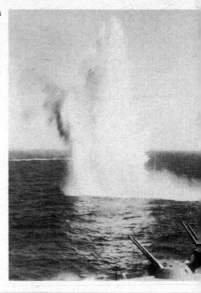

minutes when the straps holding the long range fuel tank to the fuselage of L5Q snapped. As a bomber and not a torpedo-carrying aircraft, the tank had been secured externally and not in the Observer's cockpit. Moments later it fell off into the sea, the engine cut and the aircraft rapidly lost height. By skilful airmanship Morford, the Pilot, nursed it round, restarted the engine and, although greeted with gunfire as he approached the carrier, he fired a recognition signal which caused it to cease and he landed on safely.

By 2250 the sky had cleared and Hale took his formation up to operational height at 8,000 feet (2,438 m) and twenty minutes later he sighted the colourful pyramid of flak still being projected skywards by the Taranto defences. His Observer, Carline, fixed his position from the feeble beam of the lighthouse on Cape Santa Maria di Luca on the eastern arm of the Gulf as they approached, keeping about fifteen miles off shore. The noise of their engines, picked up by the sensitive Italian airphonic listening posts, stirred the crews of the A/A batteries to even greater exertions, although the aircraft were not yet within range of their guns and the shells burst harmlessly in the air. At 2350 Hale turned north-eastwards and five minutes later detached the two flare droppers, L5B with Lieutenant R. W. V. Hamilton RN as Pilot and Sub-Lieutenant (A) J. R. Weeks RN as Observer, and L4F with Lieutenant (A) R. G. Skelton RN as Pilot and Sub-Lieutenant (A) E. A. Perkins RNVR as Observer. The gunfire had momentarily subsided but, as these two aircraft skirted the eastern shore, it recommenced. Hamilton dropped his sixteen flares at fifteen second intervals and Skelton reinforced them with eight more. Then the two aircraft made for the oil storage depot, bombing it from different directions and starting a small fire, before they set course for a return to the carrier.

The five torpedo-armed aircraft were now skirting the northern shore of the harbour and were being subjected to the full fury of gunfire aimed at them by the batteries ashore, supplemented by that of the ships themselves. Aircraft L5A (Hale) passing over Cape Rondinella at 5,000 feet (1,524 m) began to dive, jinking from side to side in an effort to avoid the hail of flak being directed towards it. The air was full of the reek of smoke from the enormous quantity of explosive which had been detonated during and after the first attack and it filled the throat and nose. Calmly, Hale selected the *Littorio* as his target and, when only 30 feet (9·1 m) above the water, he drove straight at her, releasing his torpedo at a range of 700 yards

(640 m). He then banked steeply to starboard and, narrowly missing the cable of a barrage balloon, safely made his escape.

Aircraft E4H, with Lieutenant G. W. Bayley RN as Pilot and Lieutenant H. J. Slaughter RN as Observer, followed the strike leader over Cape Rondinella, but its subsequent fate is not known as neither of the two officers were ever seen again. The Italian report of the action mentions an aircraft as shot down just west of the cruiser *Gorizia* and this may well have been the one.

Aircraft L5H, with Lieutenant (A) C. S. C. Lea RN as Pilot and Sub-Lieutenant (A) P. D. Jones RN as Observer, also followed the strike leader's aircraft but, finding the flak unpleasantly disturbing, turned a complete circle to starboard, and, losing height by this astute manoeuvre, got in beneath it. As he skimmed over the water on the northern shore he saw a Cavour class battleship beam on and released his torpedo at a range of about 800 yards (732 m). It struck the ship, the *Caio Duilio*, on her starboard side abreast 'B' turret at a depth of $29\frac{1}{2}$ feet (9 m). Narrowly missing the mast of a fishing boat, Lea took his aircraft between the cruisers *Zara* and *Fiume*, the guns of which were firing steadily at him, and then made good his escape over the northern tip of San Pietro Island.

Aircraft L5K, with Lieutenant F. M. A. Torrens-Spence RN as Pilot and Lieutenant A. W. F. Sutton RN as Observer, followed the other aircraft over Cape Rondinella and dived steeply through a veritable inferno of flak, aiming for a position five cables (914 m) south of the Canal entrance. After he skilfully avoided a near collision with the unlucky E4H (Bayley and Slaughter), Torrens-Spence found himself in the midst of a confusing armada of ships, the guns of which seemed to be concentrating on his fragile 'stringbag'. Coolly selecting a Littorio as his target, he flew towards her and at 700 yards (640 m) he released his deadly load. While getting away, the aircraft's undercarriage hit the water, but with superb skill he guided it up between two barrage balloons and out across the harbour. However his ordeal was not yet over. Two floating batteries suddenly loomed up in the water ahead too late to be avoided. He jerked back the joystick, the aircraft rose abruptly and passed over them as the guns opened fire. They were so close that the airmen could feel the hot blast of the discharge, but by little short of a miracle, they escaped with only one bullet hole in the fuselage.

Aircraft E5H, with Lieutenant (A) J. W. G. Welham RN as Pilot and Lieutenant P. Humphreys EGM, RN as Observer, had chosen a route more to the north-east of Cape Rondinella. Passing over the Mar Piccolo and the town of Taranto, Welham turned to starboard, skirting the balloon barrage on the eastern shore. Up to that moment it seemed that his presence had not been observed, but suddenly heavy machine guns opened up on him and his outer aileron was hit causing him to lose control temporarily. When he regained it, he found himself in the middle of a square formed by four of the enemy's battleships and not in a good position to fire at any of them. Some very quick thinking was necessary and he decided to aim at one of the two Littorios. He launched his torpedo from 500 yards (457 m) on the *Vittorio Veneto*'s port quarter and, turning sharply to starboard, he made his getaway under an intense hail of fire. A 40 mm shell hit the port wing and exploded, shattering some of the ribs and making a large rent in the fabric but Welham flew on and reached the *Illustrious* safely.

Aircraft L5F, which we last heard of being returned to the hangar for repairs after its unfortunate collision with L5Q just before take off, thanks to herculean efforts on the part of the fitters and riggers, had been made serviceable again in the incredibly short time of twenty minutes. As a result of eloquent pleading by the Pilot, Lieutenant E. W. Clifford RN and his Observer, Lieutenant G. R. M. Going RN, Captain Boyd gave them permission to follow the remainder of their flight on their own. They took off 24 minutes after the others and made a landfall five miles east of the harbour entrance. They had a grandstand view of the pyrotechnic display being put up for the benefit of their flight mates as they headed north-west over the town and dockyard. They could see from the oil streaked water and several fires that the enemy had taken a hard knock. The A/A barrage had died down and Clifford unhurriedly circled around looking for a suitable target to bomb. Dropping down to 2,500 feet (762 m) he dived across the line of ships and was greeted with a burst of fire. At 500 feet (152 m) he levelled off and aimed his six bombs at two cruisers, but no explosions resulted and he thought he had missed. In fact one of the semi armour piercing bombs had penetrated the thin plating of the cruiser *Trento* without exploding. Clifford then turned north, crossing the Mar Piccolo, before turning to starboard and out over the coast five miles east of the harbour entrance.

To Admiral Lyster and Captain Boyd the long wait for the return of the striking force was an agony of suspense. Although by no means a desperate venture, it was certainly a hazardous one and the price exacted might well prove to be heavy. Promptly at 0100 the *Illustrious* reached the recovery position 'Y' and headed into the wind at 21 knots. The radar might be expected to give the first indications of the return of the aircraft and, sure enough, at 0112 the operator began to notice one blip after another appearing on his screen. He passed the information to the bridge and in a moment the flight deck began to hum with activity as fitters and riggers tumbled out on deck and fire and crash parties assembled their gear.

The first to identify itself was aircraft L4C (Sparke and Neale) which landed on at 0120. The remainder of the first strike, minus their leader, followed at short intervals, Robertson carefully counting the score. Last to land on were Patch and Goodwin in E5A, the navigation lights of which had failed, but they touched down successfully at 0155. It seemed almost unbelievable that only one of the twelve aircraft had been lost. No one knew what had befallen L4A (Williamson and Scarlett) but it was sincerely hoped that they had been picked up. Quickly the deck was cleared for the second strike, only just over an hour behind the first one, but at 0155, just as Patch and Goodwin touched down, Hale and Carline in E5A sighted the carrier and landed on five minutes later, to be followed seconds later by Skelton and Perkins in L4F. Fifty minutes later Clifford and Going in L5F, the last of the second strike touched down. Again the count showed only one aircraft, E4H (Bayley and Slaughter) to be missing. Considering the strength of the defences, the casualties were far less than anyone had dared to expect. Moreover, from the modest reports of the aircrews, it was difficult at first to discover the extent of the success which had, in fact, been achieved.

CHAPTER FIVE

Taranto Night and its Aftermath

To Commander Bragadin on duty in the Operations Room of Supermarina, it had indeed been a night to remember. As the dramatic events unfolded, "news began to arrive by telephone from Taranto" he has recorded, "news that grew more serious and surprising".★ When Admiral Cavagnari was alerted he went down to the Operations Room to see for himself what was happening. A stream of messages poured in and it was quickly evident that this was not a hit and run raid but a determined attempt to cripple his fleet. At first it was not possible to gauge the magnitude of the disaster beyond that at least three of the battleships had been torpedoed and that other damage had been inflicted on smaller ships and installations. All this had been done in spite of the anti-torpedo nets, the barrage balloons and the A/A batteries.

At Taranto itself, there was stupefaction at the blow which had been delivered. As damage control parties attempted to deal with the flooding in the stricken ships and others were fighting fires, Admiral Riccardi and his staff were busy mobilising all the salvage resources of the dockyard and despatching tugs and repair parties to those ships in need of assistance. Despite urgent requests from Supermarina for a detailed report of the damage, this was not forthcoming until the following morning and when it did, it was not pleasant reading. The battleship *Littorio* had sustained three torpedo hits, two of them during the first attack, of which the one on the starboard bow had blown a hole 49 feet × 32 feet (15 m × 9¾ m) in the bulge abreast Number one 6 inch (152 mm) gun turret. The other, on the port quarter abreast the tiller flat, had made a hole 23 feet × 5 feet (7 m × 1½ m). During the second attack a third torpedo struck low down on the starboard side, just forward of the first hit, blowing a hole 40 feet × 30 feet (12 m × 9 m) in the bottom plating. A dent on the starboard quarter might, it was thought, have been made by

★ Commander Bragadin: ibid, p. 45.

another torpedo which failed to explode and which was subsequently found embedded in the mud beneath her. The ship was badly down by the bows and the forecastle partly awash. She would be out of action for a considerable time.

The battleship *Caio Duilio* had received one torpedo hit low down on the starboard side abreast of Number one 5·25 inch (133 mm) gun mounting. It had blown a hole 36 feet × 23 feet (11 m × 7 m) between numbers 1 and 2 magazines which, as a result, were completely flooded and she had had to be beached. Most serious was the damage done to the battleship *Conte di Cavour*. She had been hit on the port bow under the foremost turret during the first attack. The torpedo had blown a hole in the ship's side measuring 40 feet × 27 feet (12 m × 8¼ m) and, as a result, numbers one and two oil fuel tanks were flooded and so were the adjacent compartments. She had been towed towards the shore during the night and abandoned at 0545/12 after which she had quietly settled. By 0800 almost the whole of her upper deck was submerged including the after turret. The Italian casualties had been comparatively light, amounting to 23 men killed on board the *Littorio*, 16 in the *Conte di Cavour* and one in the *Caio Duilio*.

When daylight came, the Mar Grande presented a distressing sight with its surface covered by a film of oil. The *Littorio* was surrounded by salvage vessels as strenuous efforts were made to save her. A submarine had been brought alongside to provide electrical power and a tanker on her port quarter was receiving oil fuel as it was pumped out of her tanks to counteract the flooding.

The Mar Piccolo, too, was covered in oil which had leaked from the damaged tanks of the cruiser *Trento*. Although the bomb which struck her had failed to explode, she had a large hole in her main deck, and bulkheads and ventilation trunking had been damaged by blast. The destroyer *Libeccio* had a fractured bow as the result of a near miss and the hull of the destroyer *Pessagno* had been damaged from the same cause. Firemen were still pouring water on the smouldering ruins of the seaplane hangar. In his office Admiral Riccardi was presiding over a conference convened to reconstruct the events of the night and to draw up the report so anxiously awaited by Supermarina.

The destroyer *Fulmine* had been ordered to move at dawn from the Mar Grande to the Mar Piccolo, together with some other ships. She had on board Lieutenant Commander Williamson RN and

Lieutenant Scarlett RN whose aircraft, L4A, had been shot down and crashed into the harbour during the first attack. They had managed to extricate themselves from the sinking Swordfish and to swim to a floating dock about 150 yards (137 m) from where they had surfaced. They were rescued by dockyard workers, who gave them a rough time, but took them to the *Fulmine*, where they were well cared for until taken ashore after the ship had shifted berth. They were eventually transferred to a Prisoner-of-War camp at Sulmona, but, following Italy's surrender in 1943, they were moved to Germany where they spent the rest of the war. Of the crew of the other Swordfish lost during the attack, E4H, the body of the Pilot Lieutenant G. W. Bayley RN was recovered and buried with full military honours in the cemetery at Taranto, but subsequently moved to the Imperial War Graves Commission's cemetery at Bari. Lieutenant Slaughter's body was never found.

However, apart from the crippling effect of the raid, what worried the Italian High Command was how a British carrier or carriers had managed to approach to within striking distance of the main naval base without being detected by air reconnaissance. As Commander Bragadin remarks "At Supermarina it was taken for granted that if British forces should come within 180 miles operating range of their torpedo planes from Taranto, the Italian forces would sortie to engage the British and prevent them launching an air attack on the harbour",* but he does not explain why they were not sighted. To understand the reason, it is necessary to go back to the operations which preceded the execution of Operation 'Judgement'. On almost every occasion when Italian reconnaissance aircraft endeavoured to shadow Admiral Cunningham's fleet, they were either shot down or chased away by the Fulmar fighters flown off the *Illustrious*. On November 8th a reconnaissance aircraft had been shot down and seven S.79 bombers, which tried to get into position to attack, were turned back while still 35 miles away, one of them being shot down and another damaged. The following day, another reconnaissance aircraft was destroyed and yet another on November 10th, and a bomber formation broken up as well. In fact local air superiority over the fleet was obtained and this was a vital factor in the success of the whole operation. Describing the events, Admiral Cunningham remarks "The Fulmars were again very busy drawing off and shooting down shadowers with complete success. One of the most

* Commander Bragadin: ibid, p. 46.

important requirements of the plan was an unobserved approach to the flying off position".*

The failure of their air reconnaissance was not lost on the Italian High Command as Commander Bragadin remarks "The events of the night of November 12, added to many other lessons, confirmed in the most obvious way the very critical deficiencies of Italian air reconnaissance. The fact was that large groups of enemy ships had been cruising the whole preceding day in the central Mediterranean and, at sundown, had crossed the Ionian and Adriatic Seas; yet the Italian reconnaissance had not given the slightest warning of their presence".†

To Admiral Bernotti "The success of the air attack against the Italian fleet in the outer anchorage of Taranto was the first example of the formidable potentialities of torpedo aircraft against large ships in strongly defended bases and confirmed in general the capabilities of aircraft carriers".‡ He went on to point out that the defences of the anchorage had been shown to be insufficient partly because the A/A defences were incomplete, but principally because the anti-torpedo nets were only 8 m (26 ft 3 ins) deep, while the torpedoes were set to run at 10 m (33 ft). This was made possible by the employment of the Duplex pistols which came as a complete surprise to the Italians.

In addition to the attack on Taranto, the night had brought yet another blow. Force 'X', under Vice Admiral Pridham Wippell, comprising the cruisers *Orion* (flagship), *Sydney*, *Ajax*, and the Tribal class destroyers *Nubian* and *Mohawk*, which it will be remembered had been detached during the afternoon of November 11th, proceeded at high speed towards the Straits of Otranto. Its object was the interception of the Italian convoy which was known to run nightly across the Adriatic from Otranto, Brindisi and Bari. Passing south-west of the island of Corfu at 2030, Force 'X' steered to the northward at 25 knots until 2230 when speed was reduced to 20 knots. The sea was calm, wind force 1, sky about 7/10ths clouded and the moon in the south west, about three-quarters full. On account of the bright moonlight, the Admiral kept his force concentrated and it escaped detection. It had sufficient time to reach the line between

---

* Admiral Cunningham: ibid, p. 284.
† Commander Bragadin: ibid, p. 48.
‡ Admiral Romeo Bernotti: *La Guerra sui Mari nel Conflitto Mondiale*, p. 221.

Brindisi and Valona, but not that between Bari and Durazzo, and there was only half an hour in which to deal with any ships sighted before the force would be obliged to withdraw in order to reach a prudent distance from the enemy air bases by daylight.

By 0100/12 Force 'X' had reached the northern limit and turned round when, at 0115, the destroyer *Mohawk* on the port bow of the *Orion*, sighted some darkened ships bearing 120° distant about 8 miles. They were an Italian convoy of four merchant ships escorted by the *Nicola Fabrizi*, a torpedo boat of 650 tons armed with four 4 inch (102 mm) guns, accompanied by an auxiliary vessel, *Ramb III*, of 3,667 tons, en route for Brindisi. The *Mohawk* made the Alarm signal to her sister ship *Nubian* and closed the enemy at 25 knots. Selecting the torpedo boat as target, she opened fire at 0125 at a range of 4,000 yards (3,658 m), hitting her with her fourth salvo. The enemy ship turned away making smoke.

The *Orion* had also sighted the enemy ships and altered course across the bows of the convoy, opening fire on the third ship with her eight 6 inch (152 mm) guns at 0128, while simultaneously engaging the torpedo boat with her dual purpose 4 inch (102 mm) guns at a range of about 6,400 yards (5,852 m). The merchant ship quickly burst into flames and one of two torpedoes aimed at her struck and she was seen to sink. The scene was now illuminated by starshell and *Orion* shifted her fire to the fourth ship, which was hit repeatedly and set on fire. After being abandoned by her crew she was torpedoed and sank by the stern.

The cruiser *Ajax*, which had sighted the convoy at 0125, engaged the torpedo boat five minutes later, but she passed astern and out of range, and so fire was shifted to one of the merchant ships, which was set ablaze. She then engaged the remaining one, which, being hit by two salvos, appeared to be sinking; a torpedo fired at her missed.

The cruiser *Sydney*, the last ship in the line, had sighted the convoy as early as 0121. She opened fire on the leading merchant ship, but after she was seen to be burning, the *Sydney* shifted her fire to the second one which appeared to turn away with shells bursting all around her. Next the hapless torpedo boat, now making smoke, came within range, but quickly drew too far ahead, and so fire was concentrated on the ships of the convoy now bunched together. The *Sydney* had a lucky escape when a torpedo passed under her at 0140. She was now firing at a merchant ship lying stopped and on fire and she fired two torpedoes at another one. The *Mohawk* and *Nubian* had also been busy. The former, after her brief action with the torpedo boat engaged the second merchant ship from the left, while the latter opened fire on a merchant ship at 0131 and when she was seen to be on fire, she shifted to another one.

At 0153 Admiral Pridham Whippell broke off the action and signalled his force to steer 166° at 28 knots. During the engagement he had received a report emanating from the British Naval Attaché at Ankara to the effect that the Italian fleet intended to carry out a bombardment of the island of Corfu. As this could result in his being cut off by a stronger force than his own, and since the convoy and its escort appeared to have been destroyed, there was nothing to be gained by remaining in the area. Although not known for certain at the time, the four merchant ships viz. *Catalani* (2,429 tons), *Capo Vado* (4,391 tons), *Premuda* (4,427 tons), and *Antonio Locatelli* (5,691 tons), all sank. The *Nicola Fabrizi* was severely damaged but managed to reach port, while the *Ramb III* escaped undamaged. In his official despatch, Admiral Cunningham subsequently commented "The raid . . . was a boldly executed operation into narrow water where the enemy might well have been expected to be encountered in force. It succeeded in doing considerable damage to the enemy and undoubtedly had considerable moral effect." By noon on November 12th, Force 'X' had rejoined the Commander in Chief who was cruising in a position between Greece and Sicily about 250 miles from the Italian coast.

On board the *Illustrious*, steaming at high speed to rejoin the Commander in Chief and the rest of the fleet, there was a natural feeling of elation, but it would not be possible to assess the results of the attack until air reconnaissance had obtained photographs of the harbour. The air crews themselves, in the pandemonium reigning over the anchorage during their attacks, did not have the opportunity to observe fully the results of their efforts. However, enough had been seen to leave no doubt that the operation had been a success. Just before 0700/12, as the carrier hove in sight, a two flag hoist fluttered to the flagship's mast head underneath *Illustrious*'s pennants which was quickly translated into 'Manoeuvre Well Executed', the Royal Navy's traditional way for a Flag Officer to say 'Well Done'.

The fleet was still within range of Italian air reconnaissance aircraft, so the *Illustrious*'s Fulmars at once resumed their task of shooting down the slow Cant 501 flying boats, which attempted to sight and report it. In the words of Admiral Cunningham: "The

(the Italians) did not have much luck, for three Cant flying boats were quickly shot down by the *Illustrious*'s fighters. The last air battle took place over the fleet and we saw the large bulk of the Cant dodging in and out of the clouds with three Fulmars diving in after her. There could only be one end, and presently a flaming meteor with a long trail of black smoke fell out of the sky and splashed into the sea just ahead of the fleet. One could not help feeling sorry for the Italian airmen who had undertaken such a hopeless task in their unwieldy aircraft".★

Meanwhile, on board the *Illustrious* arrangements were going ahead to repeat the attack that evening, an action which the Commander in Chief had approved after receiving a signal from Lyster, in which he recommended that this should be done before the enemy had had time to strengthen his defences. However by 1600 Admiral Cunningham began to question the wisdom of demanding such further exertions from the carrier air crews. As one of them is reported to have remarked "After all, they only asked the Light Brigade to do it once", but he left the decision to Lyster. The matter was settled by an unfavourable weather forecast at 1800 and an obvious deterioration in the weather in the area, which caused Admiral Cunningham to cancel the repeat operation and lead his fleet back to Alexandria, which was reached on November 14th.

The first information derived from photographs taken of Taranto by the invaluable Maryland aircraft was received on the evening of November 14th from the Vice Admiral Commanding, Malta, where they were based. It reported the scene as already described and ended with the words "Hearty congratulations on a great effort". Captain Boyd, in his report, paid tribute to "the excellent photographic reconnaissance promoted by the Royal Air Force" which was an important factor in the success of the operation. The decision to use Duplex pistols in the torpedo warheads he considered justified by the results, and he went on to mention the problem facing the *Eagle*'s air crews operating from a ship with which they had not had time to familiarise themselves. He referred to the problem of the contaminated petrol, subsequently traced to the tanker *Toneline*, which had led to the loss of three Swordfish. He praised the "zeal and enthusiasm of everyone to carry out this great enterprise" and the skill of the pilots "who, in these comparatively slow machines, made studied and accurate attacks in the midst of intense anti-

★ Admiral Cunningham: ibid, p. 287.

aircraft fire". Admiral Lyster deeply regretted the unavoidable absence of the carrier *Eagle*. In a private letter he expressed the opinion that her presence "would have increased the weight of the attack considerably, and, I believe, would have made it devastating".

Admiral Cunningham described the attack in his report as "admirably planned and the determined manner in which it was carried out reflects the highest credit on all concerned". Commenting on the entire Operation MB.8, he remarked "Apart from excellent results obtained in offensive action, perhaps the most surprising feature of the whole operation was the almost clockwork regularity with which the convoys ran, ships unloaded guns and material, and with which the rendezvous of widely dispersed units were reached at the appointed time". At first the Admiralty was hesitant to believe the reports which reached it and which, due to transmission difficulties, were somewhat garbled when decyphered, but when the details were known, praise for those who had achieved such success was unstinted. The Prime Minister, Mr Churchill, with a certain amount of understandable exaggeration, told an expectant House of Commons "The result affects decisively the balance of naval power in the Mediterranean and also carries with it reactions upon the naval situation in every quarter of the globe." The First Lord of the Admiralty Mr (later Viscount) A. V. Alexander, broadcast a glowing tribute to the Fleet Air Arm. *The Times* wrote "The congratulations and gratitude of the nation are due in their fullest measure to the Fleet Air Arm, who have won a great victory in the largest operation in which they have yet been engaged against enemy ships, and to Sir Andrew Cunningham who is the first Flag Officer to handle the new weapon on such a scale and has used it triumphantly".*

On November 18th, H. M. King George VI sent Admiral Cunningham a message of congratulations in which he said "The recent successful operations of the Fleet under your command have been a source of pride and gratification to all at home. Please convey my warm congratulations to the Mediterranean Fleet and in particular to the Fleet Air Arm on their brilliant exploit against the Italian warships at Taranto".

To the surprise of his Foreign Minister and son in law, Count Ciano, Mussolini did not take the news of the disaster which had overtaken

* *The Times:* November 14th, 1940.

60

his fleet too badly. "A black day" the former recorded in his Diary, "the British, without warning, have attacked the Italian fleet at anchor in Taranto and have sunk the dreadnought *Cavour* and seriously damaged the battleships *Littorio* and *Duilio*. These ships will remain out of the fight for many months. I thought I would find the Duce downhearted. Instead he took the blow quite well and does not at the moment seem to have fully realised its gravity".*

Whether it was the attack on Taranto or the failure of Admiral Campioni two weeks later to bring a much inferior British force under Admiral Somerville to action off Cape Spartivento, which caused subsequent changes in the Italian naval commands, is not certain. The British force included the carrier *Ark Royal* and doubt-less this fact influenced the Italian Admiral's decision to avoid engagement. However, whatever the reason, on December 8th, Admiral Arturo Riccardi, formerly in charge of the base at Taranto, despite his lack of sea experience, relieved Admiral Domenico Cavagnari as Chief of Naval Staff while Admiral Angelo Iachino, formerly commanding a squadron of 8 inch gun cruisers, relieved Admiral Inigo Campioni as Commander in Chief of the Fleet, the latter being nominated Deputy Chief of Staff.

Although three of Italy's six battleships had been put out of action overnight, none of them was damaged beyond repair. The *Littorio*, the moving of which was a somewhat delicate operation on account of an unexploded torpedo in the mud beneath her, was back in operation at the end of March 1941. Repairs to the *Duilio* were completed by the middle of May, but the *Cavour*, after temporary repairs 'in situ', was not refloated until July 1941 and was then towed to Trieste where work on her had not been completed when Italy signed the armistice in June 1943. The two undamaged battleships, *Vittorio Veneto* and *Giulio Cesare*, moved the following day to Naples and later to La Spezia, where, at the end of January, they were joined by the *Andrea Doria* on completion of modernisation and working up. A division of 8 inch gun cruisers moved to Messina, but, as Admiral Bernotti points out, this redistribution of the fleet was unacceptable as a permanent measure. "By means of the aerial offensive" he wrote, "the enemy had achieved results which obliged the nucleus of our naval power to move away from southern waters, that is from the area where they were most likely to be employed, bearing in mind the necessity of disputing the movements of British

* Ciano's diary.

naval forces between the two basins of the Mediterranean".* He goes on to lament the absence of any section of the air arm charged with the duty of fleet co-operation on a permanent basis. The enforced dispersal of the fleet in the Upper Tyrrhenian Sea appeared to him to emphasise more than ever the absence of air support and meanwhile, the enemy was able to move freely in any area in which his battlefleet wished to operate.

The Italian Admiral's remarks are more realistic than some of those made at the time by Churchill and other British commentators, who were still counting battleships as evidence of naval might, whereas it was the air situation which was to dominate strategy in the Mediterranean during the ensuing years of war. The fact that Admiral Cunningham no longer had to face a superior Italian battlefleet mattered far less than the attainment of air superiority. After the attack on Taranto, for a short while, he was in the fortunate position of being able to count on this, despite the superiority in numbers of the Regia Aeronautica. However, this happy state of affairs was short lived. The misfiring of the projected German invasion against England, coupled with the failure of the Italian offensive against Greece, prompted the German Naval Commander in Chief, Admiral Erich Raeder, to renew his pleas to Hitler to turn his attention to the Mediterranean, which was to have sinister results for the British forces.

* Admiral Bernotti: ibid, p. 277.

CHAPTER SIX

The Avengers

"The co-operation of the Axis powers in the Mediterranean might have produced decisive results for the general conduct of the war had it eventuated quickly and in a timely manner, immediately after the fall of France. Instead it was invoked to deal with a disastrous situation. Objectives which could have been realised relatively easily during the first months of hostilities became more difficult as the conflict progressed because Britain had the free use of the oceans".[*] Thus Admiral Bernotti describes the situation as seen through Italian eyes as 1940 drew to a close.

On November 20th Hitler wrote his Axis partner a long letter putting forward a number of suggestions for remedying the situation in the Mediterranean. One of them was "the transfer of German Air Forces to the Mediterranean mainly to act in co-operation with those of Italy against the British fleet". Later the Führer confirmed his intention to send an Air Corps to Italy for the purpose of weakening the British naval position, but he made it quite clear that he did not, as yet, contemplate sending German troops to bolster up the deteriorating Italian position in North Africa.

First elements of Fliegerkorps X, commanded by General Geisler, began to reach Italy in December and, by early January, 330 aircraft were deployed on the Sicilian airfields of Catania, Comiso, Trapani, Palermo and Reggio Calabria. They comprised 150 Junkers 87B and 88 dive-bombers, 40 twin engine Messerschmidt 109 fighters, and 20 Dornier 18 and Arado 196 reconnaissance aircraft. All the pilots were highly experienced in operating over the sea and, in particular, in carrying out attacks against ships. The Italian Air Force could not boast of anything so formidable as the Junkers 87B (Stuka) dive-bombers, which had developed a deadly technique of getting high above their target and plummeting vertically downwards with an ear-splitting scream to release a 500 kg bomb with great accuracy.

[*] Admiral Bernotti: ibid, p. 240.

Assistance to the Greeks in their struggle against the Italians was now one of the primary tasks of the British Mediterranean fleet. In January 1941, it was decided to pass a military convoy through the Mediterranean from west to east under the code name of Operation 'Excess'. It included three ships loaded with stores for the Greek Army bound for the Piraeus and one with stores for Malta. In accordance with a practice which had now become standard, Force 'H', under Admiral Sir James Somerville, would escort the ships as far as the narrow waters between Sicily and Tunisia, they would then continue with a small escort to be met by Admiral Cunningham's fleet to the east of the Narrows, and he would arrange for their onward passage. The Commander in Chief took advantage of the occasion to organise three subsidiary convoys, one comprising two ships from Alexandria to Malta (MW.$5\frac{1}{2}$), one of two fast ships from Malta to Alexandria (ME.$5\frac{1}{2}$) and one of six slow ships from Malta to Alexandria and Port Said (ME.6). The sailing of these was timed so that MW.$5\frac{1}{2}$ made the passage under cover of the fleet as it sailed west, while the other two were to leave Malta when the fleet turned east, the two fast ships joining Convoy 'Excess' while ME.6 followed a route further to the south.

The most dangerous part of the voyage, as always, was that through the Sicilian channel, where ships were exposed to attack from enemy air bases in Sardinia and Sicily and there was a likelihood of submarine and motor torpedo-boat attack, as well as the possibility of attacks by Italian surface ships. As an extra precaution, Admiral Cunningham told Admiral Somerville that he would send the cruisers *Gloucester* and *Southampton* ahead to join up with Force 'H' south of Sardinia to provide additional escort to the convoy after Force 'H' turned back. It then had to cover 150 miles before coming under the protection of his own fleet, which, on this occasion, comprised the battleships *Warspite* (flagship) and *Valiant* and the carrier *Illustrious*, two modernised and one new ship, which he referred to as his 'First Eleven'. These would rendezvous with the convoy in a position 15 miles sout-east of the island of Pantelleria.

The dispersal forced on the Italian fleet created a demand for a much greater reconnaissance effort on the part of the Royal Air Force units, based at Malta, which it was unable to meet and, in consequence, there was some anxiety in the minds of both Somerville and Cunningham, arising from an incomplete knowledge of the whereabouts of all the Italian surface ships.

The several forces taking part in the Operation sailed according to plan and the enemy was soon aware that something was in the wind when Cunningham's fleet was sighted at sea soon after leaving Alexandria on January 7th. It was sighted again two days later, as were the cruisers *Gloucester* and *Southampton* as they were about to join up with Force 'H'. A bombing attack by ten Italian Savoia 79 aircraft that afternoon on Force 'H' was unsuccessful and two were shot down by fighters from the carrier *Ark Royal*. During the night, after Force 'H' had turned back, an attack by two Italian motor torpedo-boats was repulsed with a loss to the enemy of one of them. At 0800/10 rendezvous was made as arranged with Admiral Cunningham's fleet and soon afterwards the first untoward incident occurred when the destroyer *Gallant* had her bows blown off by a mine. While she was being taken in tow, two Italian torpedo-carrying aircraft made an unsuccessful attack. At 1030 the fleet was sighted and reported by reconnaissance aircraft, but there was, as yet, no indication of the great change which had taken place in the enemy's striking power. At 1223 two more torpedo-carrying aircraft attacked from a height of 150 feet (45·7 m), dropping their torpedoes 2,500 yards (2,286 m) from the battleships, which had no difficulty in avoiding them. Unfortunately as it happened, four of *Illustrious*'s Fulmar fighters, on patrol over the fleet, spotted the intruders and, swooping down, chased them until they were some twenty miles west of the fleet, claiming to have damaged them. The three big ships were reforming after this curtain raiser of an attack when a large formation of aircraft was reported approaching. The control in the *Illustrious* immediately recalled the fighters, ordering them to resume their overhead patrol, but two of them reported that they had used up all their ammunition and the other two had only a small amount left. So, at 1234, *Illustrious* altered course into the wind (210°) and launched four more Fulmars and two Swordfish aircraft as reliefs for the fighter and anti-submarine patrols. While this manoeuvre was in progress, two loose and flexible formations of enemy aircraft were sighted and quickly identified as German Stuka dive-bombers as they took up a position astern of the fleet at a height of about 12,000 feet (3,658 m). The avengers had arrived. Singling out the *Illustrious* as their main target, at 1238 they began their attack. Sub-flights of three aircraft peeled off to make perfectly co-ordinated attacks, one from astern and one from each beam. Sometimes they dived straight from 12,000 feet to release their bombs at about 1,500 feet (457 m), at other times they spiralled down to about 5,000 feet (1,524 m) before going into a dive and letting go their bombs, sometimes as low as 800 feet (244 m). Admiral Cunningham watched fascinated from the bridge of his flagship. "There was no doubt we were watching complete experts," he wrote. "We could not but admire the skill and precision of it all. The attacks were pressed home to point blank range, and, as they pulled out of their dives, some of them were seen to fly along the flight deck of *Illustrious* below the level of her funnel".* The carrier made drastic alterations of course in an effort to spoil the aim of her attackers but nothing short of two squadrons of fighters overhead to break up the enemy formations could have saved her.

At 1238 a 500 kg bomb went through the loading platform of Number 1 Pom-pom on the port side (n° 1—see plan 1), damaging the gun and killing two of the crew, then passing through the gun platform, it bounced off the side armour into the sea and failed to explode. A second or two later, the first direct hit (2) occurred when a 500 kg bomb landed right forward, passed through the recreation space on the port side and out through the flare of the bows to burst about ten feet (3 m) above the water line. Damage from splinters was severe and there was some consequent flooding of the forward compartments. Next a 60 kg anti-personnel bomb (3), after narrowly missing the island, scored a direct hit on Number 2 starboard Pom-pom, killing most of the gun's crew. Damage to the gun itself was slight, but ammunition in the loading trays caught fire. The jib of the mobile crane collapsed and jammed S1 Pom-pom below and electric power to both guns was cut by splinter damage and blast.

Soon after, two bombs hit almost simultaneously; they were either two of 250 kg or one 250 kg and one 500 kg. One (4) hit the lip of the after lift well at the starboard foremost corner, penetrated the lift and exploded on the floor of the lift well. The other (5) hit the lift platform near the edge on the port side and exploded. The lift, at the time, was half-way between C hangar and the flight deck with a Fulmar fighter, in the cockpit of which the Pilot, a midshipman, was sitting. The combined effect of these two bomb hits was devastating. The aircraft disintegrated and the Pilot was never seen again; a number of Swordfish and four Fulmars in the hangar caught fire and, due to a combination of blast and fire, the ship was gutted between frames 162 and 166 right down as far as the armour over

* Admiral Cunningham: ibid, p. 303.

the steering compartment. All the electric leads in the area were severed by flying splinters and these included not only those supplying power to the after ammunition hoists but also those to the steering motors. To make matters worse a near miss (6) off the starboard quarter occurring at the same time, caused damage to the steering gear itself as a result of flooding. The ship went out of control and began turning circles with the rudder jammed to port. Lieutenant H. R. B. Janvrin (Observer in L4P) was climbing into his Swordfish to collect a first aid kit when he felt it being picked up and hurled sideways. The fire parties quickly went to work lowering the fire screens and dealing with the fires.

At about 1242, a 500 kg bomb (7) hit the flight deck one foot to port of the centre-line and half-way between the island and the after lift. It penetrated the armour and exploded beneath it about two feet above the hangar deck, in which it made a hole about 60 feet square and set down the deck below it about four inches. This bomb caused considerable further damage. It buckled the forward lift into the shape of an arch, through which air rushed to fan the flames in C hangar and virtually blew out the after lift. The metal fire screens in the hangar were shredded and splinters from them wrought terrible execution amongst the fire parties and spray operators in the adjacent access lobbies. Fortunately the fire had not spread to B hangar, although it was affected by the blast from this hit. Damage was caused to the 4·5 inch gun ammunition hoists, one round exploding in the tray. Lieutenant H. R. M. Going (Observer in L5F), who had been watching the attack from the starboard catwalk hastened below to lend a hand. Finding that the officer in charge of the damage control party had been killed, he at once took charge and was assisted by other Pilots and Observers.

Further damage was caused by three near misses, one of which on the starboard quarter has been mentioned already. Another (8) on the port side caused a fire on the Senior Ratings mess deck and damaged lighting and power leads. A large splinter from this bomb penetrated the island structure and cut through the leads supplying the Radar, the Gyro compass repeaters and the 20 inch Signal Projectors. A third (9) near miss on the starboard side started a fire on the Royal Marines mess deck.

Amidst the bursting bombs, the flames and the smoke, the crashing of a shot down Ju 87 into the after lift well passed almost unnoticed, but its burning fuselage contributed to the holocaust caused by the bomb hits. Although the boiler and engine rooms were undamaged, the smoke and chemical fumes from the fires raging above them proved a serious hazard. These were being drawn in by the fans supplying air to the boilers and were essential for the combustion of the fuel, but they made the compartments well nigh untenable. Breathing through wet rags and drinking water from the auxiliary pumps to assuage their thirst, caused by the intense heat of the near red hot decks above them, the stokers gallantly stayed at their posts for almost two hours. Captain Boyd was to write "The courage and devotion to duty of the boiler room crew was magnificent."

By 1303 the steam steering engine had been connected up and the ship was once more under control and at 1313 speed was increased to 26 knots. At 1330, when the *Illustrious* was ten miles north-eastward of the battleships and the latter were nearly the same distance to the south of the 'Excess' convoy, due to the high speed avoiding action which they had been obliged to take, a high level bombing attack by Italian aircraft, possibly assisted by some from Fliegerkorps X, took place. Seven aircraft attacked the two battleships, seven the *Illustrious* and three the convoy from a height of 14,000 feet (4,267 m), but no hits were scored.

From the reports which were reaching him, it was clear to Captain Boyd that his ship had been grievously hurt. Tongues of flame were shooting out of the after lift well and the interior of the after part of the ship was a blazing inferno. He decided to head for Malta at his best speed, an action in which Admiral Cunningham fully concurred and he detached two destroyers to accompany her, but at 1335 the steering gear broke down again and for the next hour the carrier made erratic progress towards her destination. However by 1448, steering by main engines, she was making good a course of 110° at a speed of 14 knots. Down below, under the direction of the ship's Executive Officer, Commander (later Captain) Gerald Tuck RN, heroic efforts were being made to get the fires under control; then, at 1610 the enemy struck again. This time fifteen Junkers escorted by five fighters flew into position above the stricken ship, hoping to deliver a 'coup de grace' but thanks to warning received from the battlefleet's radar, they were met by the Fulmars which had refuelled and re-armed at Malta, and only nine of the enemy aircraft managed to get in their attack. By now, five of the six Pom-pom guns and all four of the forward 4·5 inch gun turrets were back in action. The electrical supply to the four 4·5 inch gun turrets which had been severed by the bombs bursting in the after lift well could not be restored. As before, the attacks were made from astern, from either quarter and from the starboard beam. Captain Boyd commented that "this attack was neither so well synchronised nor so determined as the previous one at 1240", but nevertheless one hit and one near miss did further damage and inflicted serious casualties. A bomb (10) believed to be of 500 kg size landed in the after lift well where it exploded on hitting the after ammunition conveyor and killed or severely wounded everyone in the wardroom flat. All the officers snatching a hasty cup of tea in the wardroom were wiped out and the whole of the after part of the ship was plunged into darkness. Many of the fire fighters were also killed but the blast blew out some of the fires. Lieutenant Going became a casualty, receiving injuries which necessitated the amputation of a leg. A few moments later, a near miss (11) close to the stern added to the flood damage in the steering compartment and killed everyone in the temporary sick bay which had been rigged up on the quarter deck. Another near miss (12) exploded in the sea, abreast of the island but inflicted only superficial splinter damage.

By 1631, the last of the enemy had disappeared, but the fight to get the fires under control continued and was not finally won until long after the ship berthed in Malta dockyard. At one time the flames were threatening one of the magazines and Captain Boyd was asked for permission to flood it. It was a difficult decision to make, but, with the possibility of further attacks to come, he decided to take the risk, and he was fully justified, as, at 1920, when the smoking and battered ship was only five miles from the entrance to the Grand Harbour, the enemy made a final attempt to sink her. It was an hour after sunset and the moon was up when two torpedo bombers approached from seaward. They were met with a barrage of fire from the carrier and her two escorts which kept them at a safe distance, and the torpedoes, if dropped, were not seen. In charge of three tugs, the *Illustrious* passed St Elmo light on the breakwater at 2104, and at 2215 she made fast to Parlatorio wharf.

She had received, in all, seven hits, of which one failed to explode and another exploded outside the ship's structure, five near misses and one crashed aircraft. It was most fortunate that the bomb hits were not more evenly distributed along the flight deck and strange that the after lift well seemed to have such a fatal attraction for them. The four bombs which virtually wrecked the after part of the ship had all struck unarmoured surfaces, and the one bomb that did penetrate armour did so abaft the machinery spaces. Her watertight integrity was only affected by splinter holes. The damage to the steering gear caused a good deal of inconvenience but nothing more, and the damage control organisation functioned magnificently throughout the ordeal. Without the "devotion to duty" of the boiler room personnel, the ship might well have been brought to a standstill at a critical time.

The bombing attacks, however, had taken a heavy toll of the carrier's gallant ship's company. Eighty-three officers and men had been killed, 60 seriously and 40 slightly wounded. Amongst the Taranto air crews who lost their lives were Lieutenant N. McI. Kemp RN, Pilot of L4K, Lieutenant (A) R. G. Skelton RN and Sub-Lieutenant (A) E. A. Perkins RNVR, Pilot and Observer respectively of L4F, the former dying of wounds two days later. Lieutenant E. W. Clifford RN, Pilot of L5F, Sub-Lieutenant (A) A. Mardel-Ferreira RNVR, Observer of L4H, Sub-Lieutenant (A) A. L. O. Wray RNVR, Observer of L4R were also killed, the last named dying of wounds received. As previously mentioned, Lieutenant G. R. M. Going RN, Observer of L5F, lost a leg as a result of his injuries and Lieutenant (A) W. D. Morford RN was badly burned. However, a price had also been exacted from the enemy. The *Illustrious*'s Fulmar fighters added to the laurels they had already earned by shooting down some seven enemy aircraft, whilst the ship's guns claimed another six.

It was expected that the enemy would make desperate efforts to complete the task he had failed to do whilst the *Illustrious* was at sea. The attacks, however, did not begin in force until January 16th when a raid by between 60 and 70 aircraft was mounted. They scored one hit, but the damage was not serious. Further heavy raids took place on the 18th and 19th, and, on the latter day, bombs bursting on the bottom of the harbour caused a mining effect which did serious damage to the main engines, fracturing the sliding feet of the port turbines and extensively damaging the piping and brickwork in the port boiler room. The ship's side below the armour was set in by five feet and the dishing extended over 75 feet. That these attacks were not more successful was largely due to the fact that the fifteen Royal Air Force Hurricane fighters on the island had been reinforced by a further eighteen during the recent convoy operation and they, with the assistance of the *Illustrious*'s Fulmars, took a heavy toll of the attackers. Another fact which deserves mention was the way in which the Malta dockyard workers carried on with the essential repairs to the ship defying the danger from the air attacks. At last, "by dint of superhuman efforts on the part of everyone" as Admiral Cunningham says, the *Illustrious* was made fit for sea and, at 1746 on the night of January 23rd/24th she slipped out of the Grand Harbour, unnoticed by the enemy, and, heading east at 24 knots, she reached Alexandria at 1330 on January 25th, where she was accorded a tremendous welcome by the assembled ships. After some further repairs, under the command of Captain Tuck (Captain Boyd had been promoted to Rear Admiral and appointed Rear Admiral, Mediterranean Aircraft Carriers, in place of Rear Admiral Lyster), she passed through the Suez Canal and, sailing around the Cape, safely reached Norfolk, Virginia, where she was completely refitted and repaired. She had fully justified the faith of those who designed the first armoured aircraft carrier.

Epilogue

As we have seen, Britain entered World War II with insufficient carrier strength and a belief that the gun was the final arbiter in naval action. Generally speaking, in the early stages of the war, carrier-borne fighter aircraft achieved little success in long range interceptions of enemy bomber formations attacking the fleet in northern waters. In fact, it was not until mid-1940 that the technique of fighter direction was successfully developed, first by HMS *Ark Royal*, the only modern carrier in the fleet at that time, and soon afterwards by the newly commissioned carrier HMS *Illustrious* during operations in the Mediterranean. The Skuas and Gladiators in service in 1939/40 had insufficient speed for attacking the German Junkers 87 and Heinkel III aircraft which were mainly used against ships, and when the Junkers 88 came into service the British aircraft were completely outclassed.

Italy's entry into the war further high-lighted the need for a good ship-borne fighter aircraft, since it became essential to provide cover for convoys passing through the Mediterranean with troops and supplies for Malta and the Middle East, especially in the narrow neck of water between Sicily and the North African coast, which earned the name of 'bomb alley'. Fortunately, at the same time as Italy's declaration of war, a new fighter, the Fulmar, became operational and, as has been related, reached the Mediterranean in HMS *Illustrious* in August 1940. Thanks to this new aircraft, to the use of radar and to a steadily improving standard of fighter direction, the Italian bombers and later torpedo armed aircraft, achieved comparatively little success. Most important of all, however, the arrival of the Fulmars created the conditions which made the attack on Taranto possible by preventing the Italian reconnaissance aircraft from shadowing the British fleet.

The successful attack on the Italian fleet at Taranto marked the beginning of a series of events which swept away the long cherished beliefs regarding the inferiority of carrier-borne aircraft compared with those operated from land. It confirmed the Japanese belief in the possibility of attacking the American fleet as it lay in Pearl Harbour and, ironically, it paved the way for the defeat of Japan by the sea-borne air force of the United States Navy. Further, the surprisingly small number (eight) of carriers lost during the war, disposed of the bogey regarding the high vulnerability of these ships.

Almost three decades have elapsed since World War II ended, but carrier-borne aircraft still remain an integral part of any maritime force operating outside the range of shore-based aircraft. This is particularly the case in the deployment of anti-submarine forces, since the helicopter is the submarine's greatest enemy. Even the Soviet Navy, for so long reluctant to accept the need for carriers, has at last been obliged to do so in its efforts to counter the activities of submarines deployed by the navies of the West. If we exclude the use of nuclear weapons, nothing has yet diminished the value of the carrier as a mobile, floating airfield.

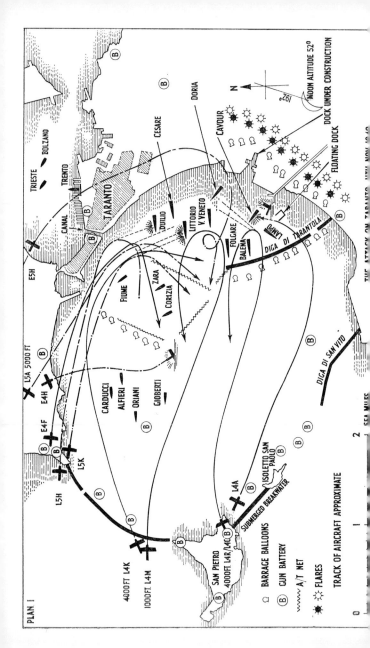

PLAN I

THE ATTACK ON TARANTO, 11TH NOV 10.40

MOON ALTITUDE 52°

1920

N

DOCK UNDER CONSTRUCTION

FLOATING DOCK

CAVOUR

DORIA

CESARE

BOLZANO

TRIESTE

TRENTO

TARANTO

CANAL

DUILIO

LITTORIO

V. VENETO

FIUME

ZARA

CORIZIA

FOLGARE

DALFNA

LANDO

DIGA DI TARANTOLA

E5H

E4H

E4F

L5A 5000 FT

CARDUCCI

ALFIERI

ORIANI

GIOBERTI

DIGA DI SAN VITO

L5K

L5H

4000FT L4K

1000 FT L4M

SAN PIETRO

4000FT L4R/L4C

ISOLETTO SAM PAOLO

L4A

SUBMERGED BREAKWATER

SEA MILES

0   1   2

Ω BARRAGE BALLOONS
Ⓑ GUN BATTERY
〰 A/T NET
☼ ❋ FLARES

TRACK OF AIRCRAFT APPROXIMATE

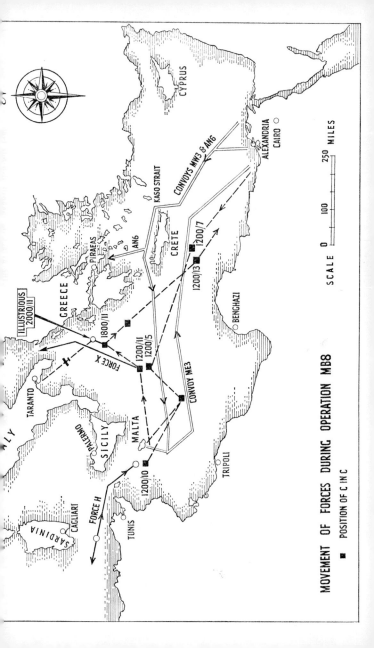

MOVEMENT OF FORCES DURING OPERATION MB8

■ POSITION OF C IN C

SCALE 0   100   250 MILES

PLAN 3

HMS ILLUSTRIOUS SHOWING BOMB HITS & NEAR MISSES ON JAN 10, 1941

SCALE

| 5 | 0 | 25 | 50 | 100 | FEET |

ILLUSTRIOUS

JU87

● BOMB HITS AND NEAR MISSES

PART II

Honours and Awards

After the praise so liberally bestowed on the personnel who took part in the attack on Taranto on November 11th 1940, it might have been expected that recognition of their gallantry would have been commensurate. However the Supplement to the London Gazette of December 20th 1940 announced the award of the DSO to the Leaders of the two strikes, Lieutenant-Commanders N. W. Williamson and J. W. Hale RN and of the DSC to their respective Observers, Lieutenants N. J. Scarlett and G. A. Carline RN as well as to Captain O. Patch Royal Marines and his Observer Lieutenant D. G. Goodwin RN, but that was all.

In the New Year's Honours List of January 1st 1941, Rear Admiral A. L. St G. Lyster received a CB and Captains D. W. Boyd and R. M. Bridge RN of *Illustrious* and *Eagle*, were each awarded a CBE.

The meagreness of the awards caused considerable ill-feeling amongst the ship's company of the *Illustrious*, especially on account of the absence of recognition of the magnificent work done by the fitters and riggers in carrying out repairs after the disastrous fire just before the attack was due to take place and ensuring that the aircraft were ready for service when required. Unfortunately by the time the attention of those in authority had been drawn to the matter, several of those whose names were to appear in a Supplementary List of Awards issued in May, had been killed during the air attack on the ship in January 1941. In this list Lieutenant G. R. M. Going RN was awarded the DSO and Lieutenants F. M. A. Torrens-Spence, C. S. C. Lea, L. J. Kiggell, R. W. V. Hamilton, H. R. B. Janvrin, A. W. F. Sutton, and Sub-Lieutenants A. S. P. Macaulay, R. A. Bailey, P. D. Jones, A. L. O. Neale, and J. R. Weekes each received the DSC. Lieutenants H. I. A. Swayne, M. R. Maund, G. W. Bayley, H. J. Slaughter and Sub-Lieutenants W. C. Sarra, and A. J. Forde RN together with eight members of the ship's company were mentioned in Despatches.

Summary of Torpedoes fired during the Attack on the Italian Fleet at Taranto, November 11th/12th 1940

Target	First Strike	Second Strike	Total Fired	Hits
Littorio	1 × 365m	1 × 640m		
	1 × 914m	1 × 640m	4	3
Veneto	1 × 1,190m	1 × 457m	2	nil
Duilio	nil	1 × 732m	1	1
Cavour	3 × 640m	nil	3	1
Goritzia	nil	1	1	nil
TOTAL	6	5	11	5

APPENDIX 3

Summary of Ammunition Expenditure by Italian Shore Defences

Cannon	125mm	1,430 rounds
	107mm	313 rounds
	88mm	6,854 rounds
Machine Gun	40mm	931 rounds
	20mm	2,635 rounds
	8mm	637 rounds
TOTAL		12,800 rounds

Ammunition expenditure by ships, the fire of which was limited to machine guns, is not known.

Fleet Air Arm Personnel taking part in the Attack on Taranto

First Strike

Aircraft & Squadron No	Name and Rank	Award
L4A 815	Lieutenant-Commander N. W. Williamson RN[1]	DSO
	Lieutenant N. J. Scarlett RN[1]	DSC
L4C 815	Sub-Lieutenant (A) P. D. J. Sparke RN	DSC
	Sub-Lieutenant (A) A. L. O. Neale RN	DSC
L4H 815	Sub-Lieutenant (A) A. J. Forde RN	M
	Sub-Lieutenant (A) Mardel Ferreira RNVR[2]	—
L4K 815	Lieutenant H. McI. Kemp RN[2]	—
	Sub-Lieutenant (A) R. A. Bailey RN	DSC
L4L 815	Sub-Lieutenant (A) W. C. Sarra RN	M
	Midshipman (A) J. Bowker RN	—
L4M 815	Lieutenant (A) H. I. A. Swayne RN	M
	Sub-Lieutenant (A) A. J. Buxall RNVR	—
L4P 815	Lieutenant (A) L. J. Kiggell RN	DSC
	Lieutenant H. R. B. Janvrin RN	DSC
L4R 815	Sub-Lieutenant (A) A. S. D. Macaulay RN	DSC
	Sub-Lieutenant (A) A. L. O. Wray RNVR[2]	—
L5B 813	Lieutenant (A) C. B. Lamb RN	—
	Lieutenant K. G. Grieve RN	—
E4F 813	Lieutenant M. R. Maund RN	M
	Sub-Lieutenant (A) W. A. Bull RN	—
E5A 824	Captain O. Patch RM	DSC
	Lieutenant D. G. Goodwin RN	DSC
E5Q 824	Lieutenant (A) J. B. Murray RN	—
	Sub-Lieutenant (A) S. M. Paine RN	—

Second Strike

Aircraft & Squadron No	Name and Rank	Award
L5A 819	Lieutenant-Commander J. W. Hale RN	DSO
	Lieutenant G. A. Carline RN	DSC
L5B 819	Lieutenant R. W. V. Hamilton RN	DSC
	Sub-Lieutenant (A) J. R. Weekes RN	DSC
L5H 819	Lieutenant (A) C. S. C. Lea RN	DSC
	Sub-Lieutenant (A) P. D. Jones RN	DSC
L5K 819	Lieutenant F. M. A. Torrens-Spence RN	DSC
	Lieutenant A. F. W. Sutton RN	DSC
L5F 819	Lieutenant E. W. Clifford RN[2]	DSO
	Lieutenant G. R. M. Going RN[3]	DSO
L5Q 819	Lieutenant (A) W. D. Morford RN	—
	Sub-Lieutenant (A) R. A. F. Green RN	—
L4F 815	Lieutenant (A) R. G. Skelton RN[2]	—
	Sub-Lieutenant (A) E. A. Parkins RNVR[2]	—
E4H 813	Lieutenant G. W. Bayley RN[4]	M
	Lieutenant H. J. Slaughter RN[4]	M
E5H 824	Lieutenant (A) J. W. G. Welham RN	—
	Lieutenant P. Humphreys EGM, RN	—

Notes
1 Taken prisoner
2 Killed during subsequent bombing of HMS *Illustrious*
3 Wounded during subsequent bombing of HMS *Illustrious*
4 Did not return from attack
M Mentioned in Despatches

Details of British Naval Aircraft

Fulmar

Two-seater carrier-borne fighter constructed by Fairey Aviation Co.
Power plant one 1,080hp Rolls-Royce Merlin VIII engine.

Dimensions Span: 46ft 4½in (14·13m); Length: 40ft 3in (13·1m); Height: 14ft (4·26m); Wing area: 342sq ft (31·77m²); Weight loaded: 9,800lb (444·52kgs)

Performance Maximum speed: 240 knots; Rate of climb: 1,200ft/min (366m/min)

Endurance at maximum speed: 2 hours

Maximum endurance: 6 hours with extra tank at cruising speed

Ceiling: 26,000ft (7,930m)

Armament Eight fixed Browning 0·303in (7·7mm) guns wing mounted

One 500lb (226·8kgs) bomb

The Fulmars of No 806 squadron embarked in HMS *Illustrious* shot down ten Italian bombers between September 2nd and October 14th 1940 and whilst giving cover to the forces engaged in the operations preceding the attack on Taranto, shot down a further six enemy aircraft. Described as "a fine aircraft, manoeuvrable, with a good take off, moderate climb and plenty of endurance"* it was not however fast enough to catch the German Junkers 87 and 88.

Skua

Two-seater carrier-borne fighter and dive bomber constructed by the Blackburn Aircraft Company, Ltd.
Power plant one 905hp Bristol Perseus XII engine.

Dimensions Span: 46ft 2in (14·5m); Length: 35ft 7in (10·8m); Height: 12ft 6in (3·8m); Wing area: 312sq ft (31m²); Weight loaded: 8,228lbs (3,732kg)

---

* British Naval Aircraft—Owen Thetford, p. 145.

Performance	Maximum speed: 196 knots at 6,500ft (1,981m)
	Initial rate of climb: 1,580ft/min (481m/min)
	Endurance: $4\frac{1}{2}$ hours; Ceiling: 20,200ft (6,161m)
Armament	Four 0·303in Fixed front guns
	One 0·303in Rear Lewis gun
	One 500lb (226·8kg) bomb

The Fleet Air Arm's first operational monoplane and dive bomber and the first to shoot down a German aircraft (Dornier Do 18) during World War II. As a fighter it lacked speed and fire power.

Swordfish

Carrier-borne three-seater torpedo-spotter-reconnaissance aircraft constructed by Fairey Aviation Company Ltd. Crew of three carried for reconnaissance work and two for torpedo attack.

Power plant one 690hp Bristol Pegasus IIIM3 or 750hp Pegasus XXX engine.

Dimensions	Span: 45ft 6in (13·8m); Length: 36ft 4in (11m);
	Height: 12ft 10in (3·9m); Wing area: 607sq ft (56·3m²);
	Weight loaded: 9,250lb (440kg)
Performance	Maximum speed: 125 knots at 4,750ft (1,447m)
	Rate of climb: 10 minutes to 5,000ft (1,524m)
	Range: 546 miles (7,16km) with a 1,610lb (730kg) torpedo
	Ceiling: 10,700ft (3,261m)
Armament	One fixed synchronised Vickers gun forward and one Vickers or Lewis gun aft. Stowage for one 1,610lb (730kg) 18in (457mm) torpedo below fuselage or two 500lb (227kg) bombs below the fuselage and two 250lb (113$\frac{1}{2}$kg) bombs below the wings, or one 500lb (227kg) bomb below the fuselage and one similar one under each wing.

The Swordfish was one of the most versatile and useful aircraft in the history of air warfare during World War II. It was generally known as the 'stringbag'. Although obsolescent when the war began it remained operational throughout the war and proved its value in Anti-submarine warfare many times over.

Details of German and Italian Aircraft

Abbreviations
G—German, MP—Monoplane, BP—Biplane, F—Fighter, DB—Dive-bomber, I—Italian, TBR—Torpedo, bomber, and reconnaissance

Description	Crew	Armament	Speed.Max/ Cruising	Range— miles
G–Me 109 F.MP single engine	1	1 × 7·9mm 2 × 20mm	317/178	655
G–Me 110 F.MP twin engine	2	4 × 7·9mm 1 × 20mm	328/160	1,200
I–CR 42 F.BP single engine	1	2 × 12·7mm	262/132	690
G–Ju 87D DB.MP single engine	2	2,000lb of bombs 4 × 2·79mm	204/159	670
G–Ju 88 TBR MP twin engine	4	5,000lb of bombs 5 × 7·9mm 1 × 20mm	249/180	1,900
G–He 111 TBR MP twin engine	5/6	7 × 7·9mm 2 × 20mm	218/166	1,930
G–F.W 200 TBR MP four engines	5/7	900lb of bombs 20mm turret 1 × 7·9mm	213/147	2,700

I–S.79 MP three engines	4/5	2,500lb of bombs 3 × 12·7mm 1/2 7·7mm	227/136	1,700
I–Cant 501 MP single engine flying boat	4/5	4·77mm	134/72	2,700

Ship's Data (British)

HMS *Illustrious*—aircraft carrier

Captain Denis W. Boyd DSC *Royal Navy*
Displacement: 23,000 tons
Dimensions: length 673ft (205m) pp 743ft 6½in (226m) oa
   beam 95ft 9in (29·2m). Freeboard to top of flight deck 42ft 2in (13m)
Draught: 24ft (7·3m)
Propulsion: Geared turbines, 3 shafts SHP 111,000   Oil fuel 4,640 tons
Speed: 30 knots
Protection: Main belt 4½in (114mm)   Hangar sides 4½in (114mm)
   Flight deck 2½–3in (63–76mm)
Armament: Sixteen 4·5in (114mm) DP guns (8 × 2) 400 rounds per gun
   Forty-eight 2 pdr A/A guns (6 × 8) 1,800 rounds per barrel
   Eight 20mm A/A guns (8 × 1) Four 0·5in Machine guns
Aircraft: 36. 24 Swordfish T.S.R. 815 and 819 squadrons, 12 Fighters
   (8 Skuas, 4 Fulmars) 806 squadron, Aircraft torpedoes 45, Petrol
   50,000 gallons, One accelerator
Builders: Vickers Armstrong, Barrow. Launched April 5th 1939,
   Commissioned April 16th 1940
Complement: 1,392

Remarks on *Illustrious's* Protection

The expectation that British carriers would be required to operate in
waters to which German and Italian shore-based aircraft would have
easy access and which the Royal Air Force was not strong enough

to dominate, was taken into account by the Admiralty when the design of the new carriers was considered in 1936. On the recommendation of the Controller of the Navy, Rear Admiral R. G. Henderson, it was decided to incorporate a considerable amount of armour protection at the expense of the number of aircraft which could be carried. This proved to be a very sound decision and the final design which was approved by the Board of Admiralty on July 21st 1936 reflects great credit on the Director of Naval Construction, Sir Stanley Goodall and his staff. The Illustrious class differed from the only post war built carrier HMS *Ark Royal*, by having a hangar which was virtually an armoured box within the hull. It was sited beneath a flight deck of 3in (76mm) armour, considered proof against a 500lb (227kg) bomb dropped from a height of less than 7,000ft (2,134m), or a 1,000lb (453·6kg) armour piercing bomb dropped from a height of less than 4,500ft (1,373m). The hangar sides and ends were made of 4in (102mm) armour and the lifts, of which there were two on the centre line, one forward and one aft, were provided with armoured shutters. The main deck below the hangar deck was of 3in (76mm) armour and covered the machinery spaces, magazines and fuel stowage. The side armour which extended down from the level of the hangar deck to 5ft (1½m) below the standard water level, was 4½in (114·5mm) thick and covered 300ft (91m) of the midship section of the ship and known as the citadel. Where the belt ended a 2½in (63·5mm) transverse armoured bulkhead was fitted both forward and aft. The bulkheads of the steering gear compartment were also made of 2½in (63·5mm) armour and overhead a 3in (76mm) deck was fitted which extended forward to overlap the armoured flight deck above it.

The ship was fitted with anti-torpedo compartments inside the hull along the length of the citadel. These were designed to absorb the shock of the explosion of a 750lb torpedo warhead. The risk of a petrol fire was minimised by stowing aviation spirit in cylinders inside tanks filled with water.

Remarks on Radar
The *Illustrious* was fitted with Type 79 (Air Warning) radar only and her completion was delayed two months in order that it could be installed.

The Mediterranean fleet as a whole, after the arrival of reinforcements in August 1940 was quite well equipped in this respect. The battleship *Valiant*, the cruiser *Ajax*, and the A/A cruisers *Coventry* and *Calcutta* all had Type 79 or 279, while the cruisers *Berwick* and *Glasgow* both had Type 286, so that during operation MB.8 there were fifteen radar fitted ships at sea with the fleet.

APPENDIX 8

Ship's Data (Italian)

As a result of the Washington Treaty on the Limitation of Naval Armaments signed in 1922, Italy was entitled to begin capital ship construction up to a total of 70,000 tons in 1927. Instead, however, of availing itself of this opportunity to renew the battlefleet, the Italian Government decided to thoroughly modernise two of the four Cavour class, all of which had been completed during World War I. Work did not begin until 1933 and was not completed until 1937. It involved a radical transformation of the interior of each ship, which, with the exception of the hull, were virtually rebuilt and fitted with underwater protection against torpedo attack. New machinery was installed, resulting in an increase of speed to 27 knots. To compensate for the extra weight added, the main armament was reduced from thirteen guns to ten and new guns were fitted, the calibre being increased from 12in (305mm) to 12·6in (320mm) and, at the same time, a new mounting enabled the elevation to be increased to give a maximum range attainable of 36,000 yards (32,918m). The secondary armament was replaced by more modern weapons and a new Conning Tower and Director Tower were fitted. So successful was the modernisation that it was decided to carry out similar alterations in the other two ships of the class, but work on these ships was not completed when hostilities began.

Battleships	Built by	Laid down	Launched	Completed
Conte Di Cavour★	Arsenale di Spezia	10/8/10	10/8/11	1/4/15

★ Reconstructed between October 1933 and October 1937

Battleships	Built by	Laid down	Launched	Completed
Giulio Cesare★	Cantiere del Tirreno	23/6/10		29/11/13
Andrea Doria†	Arsenale di Spezia	24/3/12	30/3/13	13/3/16
Caio Duilio‡	Cantiere di Castellamare di Stabia	24/2/12	24/4/13	10/5/15

★Reconstructed between October 1933 and October 1937
† Reconstructed between April 1937 and October 1940
‡ Reconstructed between April 1937 and July 1940

Displacement: 28,700 tons standard
Dimensions: Length 577ft (176m) oa   Beam 92ft (28m)
Draught: 29½ft (8·9m)
Propulsion: Parson's geared turbines on 2 shafts SHP 85,000
Speed: Designed 22 knots, but after reconstruction 27 knots
Armament: Ten 12·6in (320mm) 44 cal (3×2 and 2×2), Twelve 5·2in (133mm) *Cavour & Cesare* (6×2), Twelve 5·2in (133mm) *Doria & Duilio* (4×3), Eight 3·9in A/A (100mm) *Cesare* only (4×2), Ten 3·5in (88mm) A/A *Doria and Duilio* (5×2), 39 A/A Machine guns
Protection: Main belt 9¾in (250mm), belt ends 5in (127mm), deck 1·6in (40mm), Conning Tower 11in (280mm) *Cavour & Cesare*, 12½in (320mm) *Doria & Duilio*. Main turrets 9¾in (250mm). Secondary turrets 5in (127mm) *Cavour & Cesare*, 6in (152mm) *Doria & Duilio*.
Complement: 1,495   *Catapults:* 2   *Aircraft:* 4

Battleships	Built by	Laid down	Launched	Completed
Littorio	Ansaldo, Genoa	28/10/34	22/8/37	6/5/40
Vittorio Veneto	San Marco, Trieste	28/10/34	25/7/37	28/4/40

Displacement: 35,000 tons standard
Dimensions: Length 774ft (235½m) oa   Beam 106ft (32·3m)
Draught: 28ft (8·5m)

Propulsion: Parsons Geared turbines on 4 shafts SHP 150,000
Speed: 30 knots
Armament: Nine 15in (380mm) (3 × 3) 50 cal, Twelve 6in (152mm)
(6 × 2) 55 cal, Twelve 3·5in A/A (88mm) (6 × 2), 40 A/A Machine
Guns 48 cal
Protection: Main belt 12in (305mm), deck 5·9in (150mm)
Catapults: 2.   Aircraft 3.
Complement: 1,600
NOTE: In the design of these ships, special attention was paid to the
vertical, horizontal, and under-water protection.

Bibliography

Taranto by Don Newton and A. Cecil Hampshire—Wm Kimber & Co Ltd

The Fleet Air Arm by John Moore—Chapman and Hall Ltd

British Naval Aircraft by Owen Thetford—Putnam & Co Ltd

Fleet Air Arm by Lieutenant Commander P. K. Kemp OBE, RN—Jenkins (Herbert) Ltd

Wings of the Morning by Ian Cameron—Hodder and Stoughton Ltd

A Sailor's Odyssey by Admiral of the Fleet Viscount Cunningham of Hyndhope KT, GCB, OM, DSO—Hutchinson & Co

Ciano's Diary Edited by Malcolm Muggeridge—Wm Heinemann Ltd

La Guerra Sui Mari Nel Conflitto Mondiale by Ammiraglio Designato d'Armata Romeo Bernotti—Societa Editrice Tirrena, Livorno

The Italian Navy in World War II by Commander M. A. Bragadin, Italian Navy—United States Naval Institute

HMS Illustrious by Kenneth Poolman—Wm Kimber

Brassey's Annual 1959 Edited by Rear Admiral H. G. Thursfield—Wm Clowes Ltd

Warship Profiles Nos 10 and 11, HMS *Illustrious*, Profile Publications Ltd, Coburg House, Windsor, Berks.

Index

Rank abbreviations:

A. of F.: Admiral of the Fleet; Ad.: Admiral; V.-Ad.: Vice-Admiral; R.-Ad.: Rear-Admiral; Comdre.: Commodore; Capt.: Captain; Cdr.: Commander; Lt.-Cdr.: Lieutenant-Commander; S.-Lt.: Sub-Lieutenant

93

7.00653